DECORATING AMERICAN STYLE

DECORATING AMERICAN STYLE

José Wilson & Arthur Leaman ASID

NEW YORK GRAPHIC SOCIETY, Boston

For their help in gathering material for this book, the authors are grateful to the following magazines:

Antiques Magazine
American Home
Better Homes & Gardens
Cosmopolitan
House Beautiful
Interior Design
Ladies' Home Journal
Redbook

and to the following people:

Miss Abby Raymond, Brunschwig & Fils
Mr. and Mrs. Edwin Bitter, Scalamandré Fabrics, Inc.
Mr. Fred Batson, Jr., The Kittinger Company
Mr. Harold A. Sparks, The Colonial Williamsburg Foundation
Miss Phyllis Daignault, Ethan Allen
Parsons School of Design Library
Society for the Preservation of New England Antiquities
Mrs. Anne Genter, Sewickley, Pennsylvania
Mrs. Marilyn Schafer, San Francisco, California
Mrs. Betty Ward, Newport Beach, California

Library of Congress Cataloging in Publication Data

Wilson, José
    Decorating American style.

    Bibliography: p. 199–200
      1. Interior decoration—United States.
2. Furniture—United States. I. Leaman, Arthur,
joint author. II. Title.
NK2002.W52   747'.213   75–363
ISBN 0–8212–0603–6

First printing

Printed in the United States of America

Composed in 11/14 Optima by DEKR Corporation, Woburn, Massachusetts
Printed by Meehan-Tooker, East Rutherford, New Jersey
Bound by A. Horowitz and Son, Clifton, New Jersey

First Edition

Printed in the United States of America

Contents

INTRODUCTION

Decorating American Style

is an amalgamation of many influences that had its genesis in the European background of the first settlers. During that greatest of all design periods, the eighteenth century, as colonial America grew, prospered, and won independence, the taste and elegance that flowed across the Atlantic found a free fresh expression in the New World. Americans have always embraced good design, no matter where it originated, and it is this readiness to accept the best the world can offer, allied to a national predilection for color, comfort, and convenience, that has resulted in what is internationally recognized as a uniquely American decorating style.

1. The updating of tradition, the vital link with the past, to fit today's living concepts is exemplified by a bedroom in Blair House, Washington, D.C., the nation's guesthouse. William Pahlmann, FASID, used antique furniture in the Victorian rococo style of Lincoln's day with authentic reproductions by Scalamandré of period fabrics and wallpaper and a reproduction of a nineteenth-century rug.
2. Vibrant colors, concentrated by designer Richard Ohrbach in a dining corner, photographed by Bill King, typify the bravura combinations of the 1970's.
3. The quintessential American room, on which the most money, time, and imagination is lavished, is undoubtedly the kitchen. In this kitchen, designed by the owner, Herbert Schiffers, an adroit and workmanlike fusion of old and new, the black-and-white checkerboard floor, a seventeenth-century design reinterpreted in vinyl tile, is the link between modern cooking equipment and an antique painted hutch and dough tray turned work table.
4. Collections are an integral part of American interiors. This room, photographed by David Massey, was designed as a light-filled space where modern American art, such as the Frank Stella painting and early Jim Dine watercolors, could be enjoyed.

1 2

3

4

List of Museums, Historic Houses, and Restorations

Houses and Restorations

COLORADO

Claude Boettscher Mansion, Denver

CONNECTICUT

Mark Twain House, Hartford

DELAWARE

William Corbit House, Odessa

FLORIDA

Juan Gallegos House, St. Augustine

GEORGIA

Owens-Thomas House, Savannah

INDIANA

Morris-Butler House, Indianapolis

LOUISIANA

Rosedown, St. Francisville

MARYLAND

Carroll Mansion, Baltimore

Hammond-Harwood House, Annapolis

MASSACHUSETTS

Abraham Browne House, Watertown

Beauport, Gloucester

General Salem Towne House, Old Sturbridge Village

Harrison Gray Otis House, Boston

Whipple House, Ipswich

Winslow-Crocker House, Yarmouthport

MINNESOTA

Alexander Ramsey House, St. Paul

NEBRASKA

Arbor Lodge, Nebraska City

William Jennings Bryan House, Lincoln

NEW YORK

Bartow-Pell Mansion, Shore Road, Bronx

Lyndhurst, Tarrytown

Sleepy Hollow Restoration, Tarrytown

NORTH CAROLINA

Liberty Hall, Kenansville

Tryon Palace, New Bern

Wright-Stanly House, New Bern

PENNSYLVANIA

Mount Pleasant, Fairmount Park, Philadelphia

Pottsgrove, Pottsville

Woodford Mansion, Fairmount Park, Philadelphia

PUERTO RICO

La Fortaleza, San Juan

RHODE ISLAND

Hunter House, Newport

Whitehall Museum House, Newport

SOUTH CAROLINA

Edmonston-Alston House, Charleston

Heyward-Washington House, Charleston

Nathaniel Russell House, Charleston

TENNESSEE

The Hermitage, Nashville

VIRGINIA

Colonial Williamsburg: Coke-Garrett House, Governor's Palace, Peyton-Randolph House, Williamsburg

Kenmore, Fredericksburg

Monticello, Charlottesville

Mount Vernon

Shirley Plantation, Richmond

Wickham-Valentine House, Richmond

WASHINGTON, D.C.

Blair House

The Lindens

The White House

TEXAS

Houston Museum of Fine Arts, Houston (Bayou Bend Collection)

ENGLAND

American Museum, Claverton Manor, Bath

Museums

DELAWARE

Henry Francis Du Pont Winterthur Museum

MARYLAND

The Peale Museum, Baltimore

MASSACHUSETTS

Museum of Fine Arts, Boston

Shaker Museum, Hancock

NEW YORK

Brooklyn Museum, Brooklyn

Metropolitan Museum of Art

Museum of the City of New York

Museum of Modern Art

PENNSYLVANIA

Philadelphia Museum of Art

1
A Rich Decorative Heritage

In less than four hundred years, America has built an impressive design tradition. Successive waves of conquerors, colonists, and immigrants brought into the virgin territory many influences, ranging from the massive carved furniture of the Dutch merchants and the monastically simple functional tables and chairs of the early Spanish missions to the naive painted pieces of the German peasant-farmers and the classically elegant eighteenth-century styles of the wealthy English aristocrats.

At first the settlers, clinging to their memories and a few treasured possessions, strove to recreate the ambiance of the homelands they had left behind. Gradually, as the rigors of battling a new and hostile environment lessened and life became more orderly, they began to fashion their own furniture, develop their own colors, weave their own fabrics, and decorate plain wood furniture and bare walls and floors with paint and pattern. Houses were built with separate rooms for sleeping, dining, entertaining, and studying. Furnishings became more luxurious, windows larger, and window treatments more elaborate; floors were fitted with custom-made carpets. In their ability to adapt and shape the vestiges of the past to the exigencies of the present, our ancestors set an enduring precedent.

With space and heat precious in the seventeenth century, families ate, slept, cooked, and socialized in the parlor, the first expression of one-room living.
1. The Jacobean-style parlor of the Abraham Browne House in Massachusetts is typical of life in early New England. The bed is curtained against drafts, a treasured Oriental rug is used to cover the table rather than being put on the dirty wood floor.
2. The parlor-bedroom from the Jan Martense Schenck House in the Brooklyn Museum shows the Dutch version of communal living. Two built-in beds flank a richly carved "kas" or wardrobe-cupboard. The chairs are upholstered in "turkey work," needlework in cut pile made in the West to simulate the look of woven Oriental rugs.

1. Photographer: Richard Merrill (Courtesy, S.P.N.E.A.).
2. (Courtesy, The Brooklyn Museum).

1

2

3

4

The Fraktur Room at Winterthur (**1**) is an outstanding example of the way regional folk-art decoration was used in the eighteenth century to transform plain woods and backgrounds. Chests and a desk-bookcase have typical Pennsylvania Dutch decoration and motifs; the paneling, painted a soft blue, is both plain and patterned. The sturdy simplicity of New England is reflected in the Pembroke Room at Beauport, Gloucester, Massachusetts (**2**), Henry Sleeper's reconstruction of the "keeping room" of his ancestors. The room is a study in warm-toned pine, from walls, floor, and ceiling to early pieces of furniture. Decoration was minimal in the austere early Spanish houses (**3**). A dark-red kickboard painted around the walls is the only color in the white-washed kitchen of the Juan Gallegos House in St. Augustine, Florida. The other side of the colonial coin, the grandeur of the Spanish rulers, prevails in the State Dining Room of La Fortaleza (**4**), the Governor's Palace in San Juan, P.R., with its hand-carved furniture and marble floor.

1. (Courtesy, The Henry Francis du Pont Winterthur Museum).
2. (Courtesy, S.P.N.E.A.).
3. (Courtesy, Historic St. Augustine Preservation Board).
4. Photographer: Gaspar Gómez, Jr.

1

As America prospered in the eighteenth century, austerity gave way to luxury. The homes of the wealthy colonists, furnished in local versions of European styles, were designed for the civilized pleasures of dining and entertaining, music, and writing.
1. The dining room of The Lindens, Washington, D.C., once the home of a Massachusetts merchant prince, bears mute witness to the prevalence of dinner parties, with its three-part table and set of twelve New York Chippendale chairs. The windows are screened with a fashion of the day—Venetian blinds.
2. Intellectual exercises are catered to in George Washington's library at Mount Vernon. The Philadelphia Hepplewhite secretary, desk chair, and London custom-made terrestrial globe were all owned by Washington.
   After the Revolution, the restraint of the eighteenth-century interior was replaced by the red-and-gold color schemes, dark-toned woods, and more grandiose furnishings of the nationalistic Federal and Empire periods.
3. A typical room of the day is the 1820's drawing room from the American Museum in Bath, England, with Duncan Phyfe furniture and caryatid mantel supports.
4. Another example is the bedroom of the Bartow-Pell Mansion in New York State, which is dominated by a massive French-style Empire bed topped with a *couronne de lit*, by Charles Honoré Lannuier.

1. Photographer: Bill Aller.
2. (Courtesy, The Mount Vernon Ladies' Association).
3. Photographer: L. Barrow (Courtesy, *Life Magazine*).
4. Photographer: Bill Aller.

4

1

2

3

American rooms of the late eighteenth and early nineteenth centuries evidence a
more social life, an eclectic taste nurtured by trade with Europe and the Orient. The
"withdrawing room" of the 1796 Harrison Gray Otis House in Boston (1) reflects the
increased use of color, pattern, and decorative background treatments. Pattern
predominates, from the fitted carpet to the caned and japanned chairs around the
tea and game tables and the wallpaper borders outlining windows, dado and
plasterwork ceiling moldings. In the Federal dining room at Bayou Bend (2),
luxurious color and pattern are introduced by a gold-leaf painted canvas wall
covering and silk damask seats on the Duncan Phyfe chairs. Unfortunately, the
grace and lightness of the initial Federal styles declined into the ponderous
heaviness of American Empire, a take-off on the styles of Napoleonic France. In the
Empire parlor at Bayou Bend (3), the window treatments are more elaborate, with
painted cornices and swagged draperies, and the furniture is ornately decorated
and gilded. The Argand lamp on the table is an innovation of the day that gave a
much brighter light than the old oil lamps.

1. (Courtesy, S.P.N.E.A.).
2, 3. (Courtesy, The Museum of Fine Arts, Houston).

Federal and American Empire were followed by a giddy succession of Victorian revivals of styles of the past. This was an age of decorative excess, of opulent fabrics, elaborate window treatments, carved and tufted furniture, gobs of gilding, and a positive forest of bric-à-brac. The zenith of the rococo revival is the Victorian parlor of the Wickham-Valentine House in Richmond, Virginia, where the Valentine Museum opened to the public in 1898. The interior of the house, which was built in 1812 along neoclassical lines, was completely re-done in the Victorian manner in the 1850's. Although some of the rooms were later restored to their original look, the trappings of the parlor—paneling, ceiling painted to simulate moldings, gilded cornices, mirrors, and gas chandelier—were left untouched. Regally surveying the room is the young Queen Victoria, in an 1839 portrait by Thomas Sully. The rococo rosewood-and-walnut sofa and medallion-back armchairs are upholstered, and the windows draped, with damask reproduced by Brunschwig & Fils from a design of the period researched by William Lee Joel II, ASID.

Photographer: Helga Studios (Courtesy, *Antiques Magazine*).

19

Among the more eccentric manifestations of the Victorian revivals were Gothic and Renaissance. Jay Gould slept in this bedroom at Lyndhurst (1), a pure example of neo-Gothic from the ribbed and vaulted ceiling and arched molding over the door to the bed, as flamboyantly carved as a medieval pulpit. His mansion on the Hudson was the *tour de force* of architect Alexander Jackson Davis, leading exponent of the style, who also designed much of the furniture for the original owner. Even the unsullied prairie states were not immune to the rash of grandeur that spread across America in the 1870's. Alexander Ramsey, second governor of Minnesota, built himself a Renaissance mansion in St. Paul, furnishing it with ponderous furniture of the same ilk (2). While the heavily carved furniture in the library of Mark Twain's Hartford, Connecticut house (3) was in the taste of the day, the background, executed by Louis Comfort Tiffany and his associates, has the elegance of Art Nouveau. Tiffany's gold stenciling on the peacock-blue walls makes an unusual setting for the mélange of patterns, objects, and furniture on which the Victorians doted.

2. (Courtesy, *Country Beautiful*, from *Great Historic Houses of America*).
3. Photographer: Meyers Studio (Courtesy, Mark Twain Memorial, Hartford, Connecticut).

2

3

1

2

3

Although the Victorians would never have admitted it, their cumbrous furniture looked best against the airy background of a room stripped down for summer, which is much the way we use it today.

1. Considered the height of fashion in the 1870's, this neo-Renaissance parlor, liberally endowed with obelisks and sphinxes, put on a fresh summer face when heavy draperies and patterned carpets were replaced by lace curtains and fitted straw matting, enabling the lines of the dark-framed purple damask-upholstered seating pieces to stand out.

2. Although the curly maple neo-Jacobean bed and dresser in this bedroom at Arbor Lodge, Nebraska, are heavily scaled, the light-toned wood makes them appear less substantial—an illusion reinforced by sheer curtains, accent rugs on a bare floor, and a fanciful bamboo nightstand.

3. The embellishments of the wealthy and worldly were not for the Shakers, whose unadorned furniture expressed their belief that form followed function. While based on traditional forms, Shaker pieces were refined to a spare, space-conserving purity of line, and much of the storage was built in. The Shakers' sole concession to decoration was the painting and staining of wood in certain prescribed colors—mustard yellow, red, reddish-orange, blue, and bottle green—and a webbing of colored worsted tapes on chair seats.

1. (Courtesy, Metropolitan Museum of Art, New York).
3. Photographer: Harry Hartman (Courtesy, The Shaker Museum, Hancock, Massachusetts).

1

2

3

Posh revivals might come and go, but rural craftsmen and artisans continued to turn out the unpretentious plain and painted country furniture which the majority of people could afford.

1. Two types of early Texas furniture are shown in a bedroom at Hatfield Plantation, Houston. The slatback chairs and pine armoire are typically American; the reeded Sheraton-style four-poster and Hepplewhite-style table are simplified versions of English designs.

2. Painted cottage furniture, mass-produced in Grand Rapids from the 1850's, with its ball and spool turnings and stenciled nosegays, was the machine-age successor to the hand-painted chests, chairs, tables, and beds produced in country areas from the late 1600's.

3. More than any other emigrant group, the Pennsylvania Dutch were masters of the art of painted decoration. They drew on their German-Swiss heritage for the naive folk-art motifs with which they embellished everyday pieces and for the simulated graining on the four-poster in this bedroom.

1. Photographer: Helga Studios (Courtesy, *Antiques Magazine*).
2. (Courtesy, Sleepy Hollow Restoration).
3. Photographer: Lisanti (Courtesy, *Good Housekeeping* and The Philadelphia Museum of Fine Arts).

1

2

DESIGN MARCHES ON—
INTO THE TWENTIETH CENTURY

Victorian taste didn't expire with Queen Victoria. It was in evidence through the first decade of the twentieth century, when something new was added—the acquisitions of globe-trotting Americans. Like many Americans abroad, William Jennings Bryan collected souvenirs of his 1905 world tour, which he displayed in the "Curio Room" of his home in Lincoln, Nebraska (1). An early example of eclectic decorating, the room holds a Hong Kong peacock chair, a copy of a Renaissance X-base chair, a Moorish table, a cluster of small Oriental prayer rugs, and numerous Eastern *objets d'art*. In the parlor (2), beside a bust of Bryan, a walnut elephant table from India keeps company with a mixture of furniture, from Queen Anne to American Empire. Between 1905 and 1917, Grand Rapids took over, turning out for American homes machinemade matched suites that were loosely based on classic styles, such as Chinese Chippendale, with some bamboo turning thrown in (3), or heavy-handed interpretations of native Mission. Oriental rugs and china cabinets were still popular. In the 1920's, there was a new craze for chintz and cretonne slipcovers as baggy and saggy as a wrapper (4). With solid-colored fitted carpet, puffy satin pillows, picture groupings, and masses of spindly little tables holding vases and signed photographs, such a room was considered the height of modernity. When suites weren't slipcovered, they were upholstered in plushy fabrics or damasks (5), and in the grander establishments, the period look lingered in cabinets painted with Watteauesque scenes, and Louis XV legs on furniture.

1, 2. Photographer: Doug Green (Courtesy, *Country Beautiful* from *Great Historic Houses of America*).
3. (Courtesy, New York Public Library Picture Collection).
4. (Courtesy, *House & Garden Book of Interiors, 1920*).

26

3

4

5

Although design in the 1930's followed many an odd byway, eventually it took the path that led to the establishment of a truly contemporary twentieth-century style.

1. Cosily but excessively furnished, the English country house look displayed its Tudor pretensions with cathedral ceilings and small-paned casement windows. In living rooms, pieces of different periods were combined, and bare polished wood floors sported real tiger rugs.

2. The California Spanish style, a rather over-powering mixture of fake beams and grillework, religious art, and elaborate accessories, was the forerunner of today's Mediterranean style.

3. Chinese Modern had more to recommend it. This harmonious and restrained room designed by Ruth Wittington, with its carved rug, gracefully rounded sofas, and display of Chinese art would hold up well today.

4. By 1936, the utilitarian bathroom had turned sybaritic show-off, sheathed in mirror, with sleekly contoured fixtures and the luxuries of a carpeted floor and chandelier.

5. The Art Deco bedroom of George Gershwin's apartment on Riverside Drive, New York, with its jazzy, angular shapes and patterns, was representative of this recently revived style.

6. The fantasy world of the movies spawned the Hollywood Modern style of furniture covered in shiny white antique satin and leather, and voluptuously tufted and padded, wood storage headboards lacquered white, with indirect lighting.

7. The shape of things to come began to emerge in 1934, when Alvar Aalto's blond laminated-wood furniture ushered in the era of Swedish Modern, which became the 1940's status symbol.

1, 3, 4, 6. (Courtesy, New York Public Library Picture Collection).
2. Photographer: Otto Maya.
5. (Courtesy, Museum of the City of New York).
7. (Courtesy, *All About Modern Decorating* by Mary Davis Gillies).

28

1

2

5

6

7

Hollywood has been one of the greatest influences on American lifestyles since the days when Cecil B. de Mille glamorized and glorified the bathroom, with tantalizing glimpses of pearly flesh rising from foam-filled sunken marble tubs watered by golden faucets.

1. The dream world of Hollywood Modern, an off-shoot of Art Deco, was born at the height of the Depression. MGM's 1933 *Dinner at Eight* and Jean Harlow's bedroom, with satin-upholstered, white-lacquered bed, a-glitter with mirrors and crystal, set a much-copied style. (A revival of Art Deco coincided with the 1965 *Harlow*, starring Carroll Baker.)

2. The blockbuster of pre-war 1939, MGM's *Gone with the Wind*, for which designer Joseph Platt was set adviser, started the taste for Civil-War period Victoriana, from simple country styles to the rococo splendors of the parlor, where Belle Watling received Rhett Butler. The table lamp became known as the GWTW lamp.

3. In Warner Brothers' 1958 *Auntie Mame*, Mame's decorative phases were as varied as her romances, ranging from Chinese Modern to the then-fashionable form of eclecticism, expressed by an offhand mingling of French furniture with a wicker-and-glass coffee table and white wall-to-wall carpet.

4. The hottest color scheme of the 1950's, pink and orange, was popularized by the Thai settings of Twentieth Century Fox's *The King and I*, a 1956 movie of the hit stage musical.

5. Another musical, successfully transposed to the screen in 1958, was *My Fair Lady*, for which Cecil Beaton designed the Edwardian costumes and sets in Art Nouveau style, which was to become a major design look of the 1960's.

6. The much ballyhooed 1963 *Cleopatra* made by Twentieth Century Fox with Elizabeth Taylor and Richard Burton stimulated a short-lived resurgence of the Egyptian look, mainly in motifs, fabrics, and decorative objects—the furniture never really caught on.

From the amusing junk decor of Holly Golightly's apartment in *Breakfast at Tiffany's*, with its old bathtub-turned-sofa, to the futuristic sets of *2001* and *A Clockwork Orange*, the movies of the last decades have exerted a strong influence on interior design, stimulating both imagination and nostalgia. With the 1920's mood and decoration of *The Great Gatsby*, we seem to have come full circle. To be in the forefront of the new-old trends, it pays to keep an eye on the movies.

1, 2. (Courtesy, Museum of Modern Art Photo Library).

30

1

2

3

4

5

6

1

2

3

The emergence in the 1940's and 50's of a distinctively modern architectural style, with wall space diminished by vast expanses of glass, inevitably altered interior decoration. This was the era of the window wall, the conversation pit, the open plan, area-defining rugs and room dividers, and mixtures of furniture that went together without looking alike, a switch from the upholstered matched suite of earlier days.

1. The inflexible window wall was one of the first of the architectural innovations to dictate decoration. In this 1950's living room designed by Melanie Kahane, ASID, the seating group gravitates toward the view, and the traditional solidarity of the upholstered pieces is tempered by modern furniture with long sleek see-through lines and a background that is simple and uncluttered.

2. Architecture is the dominant factor in the forty-foot living room of a house designed by architect Allen J. Gelbin, a disciple of Frank Lloyd Wright. The major seating piece is a banquette built in to follow the sinuous curve of the wall; the floor is paved with an architectural material, red clay tile.

3. The ultimate answer to the architect's desire to keep sight lines and space unobstructed was the conversation pit. In this house, designed by architect Paul Rudolph, furniture is virtually non-existent. Decoration derives from art, plants, natural textures, the soft wash of light, and shadow from built-in sources.

1. Photographer: Guerrero.
2. Photographer: Frederick J. Miller (Courtesy, Previews, Inc.).
3. Photographer: Ezra Stoller.

1

From the 1940's, the path of decoration led inexorably to the Age of Plastic.
1. Eclectic was the word adopted to express the new freehand mixture of styles, exemplified by this 1940's apartment designed by Yale R. Burge, where design influences from Regency to Chinese are combined against dark walls and ceiling.
2. Furniture with contoured shapes and spindly legs; woven fabrics with a textured homespun look in the newly brilliant colors pioneered by Dorothy Liebes and Boris Kroll; wall displays of graphics, posters, and folk art—these spelled modern in the 1950's, a look summed up by this living room designed by the owner, Alex Steinweiss.
3. The second half of the century brought a wave of manmade materials, many of them uncannily like their natural counterparts. In this apartment designed by Margot Gunther, ASID, almost everything is synthetic, from the nylon carpet and Naugahyde upholstery with the appearance of suede to bookshelves and tables of laminated plastic and plexiglass.
4. The trendy furnishings of the late 1960's, shown in a zingy and colorful room designed by Emily Malino, ASID, were one facet of the youth culture trend. A soft, squashy beanbag sofa for floor-level lounging, Italian modern chair and table, and a sculptural lamp are all designs conducive to a casual style of living.

1. Photographer: Hans Van Nes.
2. Photographer: Otto Maya.
3. Photographer: Darwin Davidson (Courtesy, Monarch Carpet).
4. (Courtesy, Window Shade Manufacturers Association).

2

3

4

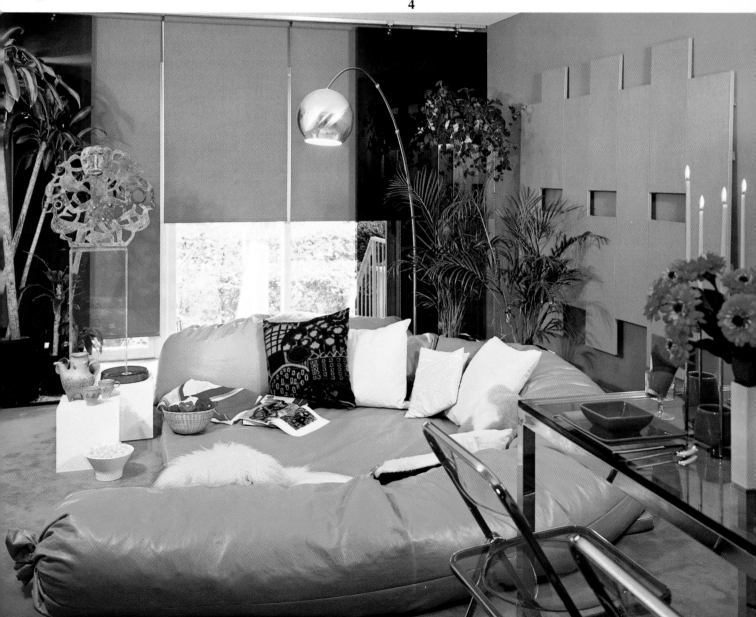

2
The Past Preserved

A remembrance of things past keeps us in touch with our heritage. Today we are richly endowed with a wealth of historic preservations, restorations, and museum recreations of traditional rooms where we can study the best of the past, and trace the emergence of a distinctively American decorating style—and lifestyle. The collections of the Rockefeller family at Colonial Williamsburg and Henry Francis du Pont at Winterthur provide a lively, encyclopaedic documentation of the development of that style. On a smaller and more personal scale we have Thomas Jefferson's Monticello, uniquely American in its inventive approach to space planning and problem solving, the great eighteenth-century houses of Tidewater Virginia, Charleston, Newport, Boston, Philadelphia, and Delaware, and the romantic plantation mansions like Shirley and Rosedown. Not only these houses, but also the smaller humbler homes of the simple country people are evidence of the vigor, vitality, and ingenuity that put an unmistakable ''made in America'' stamp on every aspect of our traditional design and decoration, even though the influences and inspiration may have originated, as they so often did, in Europe.

1. The flying staircase at Shirley, the Carter family's James River plantation mansion, rises three stories without visible means of support, an extraordinary architectural feat, considering that it was built in the eighteenth century.
2. One of the first great houses to be constructed in the colonies was the Governor's Palace at Williamsburg, Virginia. For the Colonial Williamsburg reconstruction, interiors were based on documentary evidence. The gilt, hand-tooled Spanish leather wall-covering in the Governor's study was listed in the original inventory.
3. The antebellum Greek Revival mansion of Rosedown in St. Francisville, Louisiana, with interiors restored by McMillen Inc., opened to the public in 1964. The parlor, an elegant example of 1830's fashion, has a circular Aubusson carpet, Victorian parlor set, and a needlepoint firescreen that was worked by Martha Washington.

1. Photographer: Helga Studios (Courtesy, *Antiques Magazine*).
2. Photographer: Peter Stackpole (Courtesy, *Life* Magazine).
3. (Courtesy, McMillen Inc.).

1

2

3

1

Subtle modulations of color were the hallmark of the eighteenth-century palette.

1. Soft tones of ashes-of-roses and pastel blue-green on walls, paneling, pilasters, and pediments save the drawing room in the William Corbit House in Odessa, Delaware, from excessive formality, which would have been the case had the wood been dark.

2. In the Edmonston-Alston House in Charleston, recently opened as an 1820's museum, the creamy off-white plaster and woodwork are a perfect foil for the delicate elegance of painted Sheraton-style chairs and the Empire-green glass chandelier.

3. Muted yellow paneling in the East bedroom of the Peyton-Randolph House at Colonial Williamsburg adapts to either a winter or, as here, a summer scheme, with grass matting replacing carpets, seersucker Austrian shades the blue curtains.

1. Photographer: Guerrero.
2. Photographer: Helga Studios (Courtesy, *Antiques Magazine*).
3. (Courtesy, Colonial Williamsburg).

2

3

1

When fireplaces were the only source of heat, they were the decorative focal point of a room, and frequently were faced with marble or tile, boiserie or plasterwork.
1. The plaster relief ceiling and overmantel, the latter depicting the Aesop fable of the fox and the crow, in the drawing room of Kenmore, Fredericksburg, Virginia, recall the interior glories of England's Palladian houses, undoubtedly the model for this superb example of eighteenth-century architectural detail. In those days, the aristocratic elite, like George Washington's sister, who lived here with her husband, could command the services of a "stucco man" to execute their designs.
2. Much more prevalent was the kind of simple paneled fireplace and brick hearth in this old Newport house, a type found in many houses in the northeastern states.
3. By the late nineteenth century, Newport was no longer a trading center but the playground for the Vanderbilts and their friends, who built vast neo-Renaissance palaces, deprecatingly referred to as "country cottages." Even a small reception room might be graced by boiserie imported from France and a marble fireplace, and furnished with Louis XVI antiques.

1. Photographer: Louis H. Frohman.
2, 3. Photographer: Guerrero.

2

3

1. A folk-art form of painted decoration brings pattern to one wall of a small 1830's bedroom from the Joshua La Salle House in Connecticut, now in the American Museum, Bath, England. To simulate wallpaper, wood sheathing was stenciled with a stylized motif taken from the bedcover, stenciled, like much of the furniture.

2. The contrast of pale-blue walls and deep-blue painted paneling, molding, and chair rail makes a strong decorative statement in this bedroom in the William Corbit House in Odessa, Delaware. The color scheme is accented by a chair covered in a vivid tone of pink, much as we would do it today.

3. Yet another form of decoration was the landscape in oils that was often set into a carved and painted overmantel, like a permanently framed picture. The pale aqua tint of the paneled walls in the drawing room of the Woodford Mansion in Philadelphia blends with the lighter tone of the marble fireplace in a subtle color scheme that is sharpened only by the red upholstery of the wing chair.

4. One of the finest examples of eighteenth-century painted decoration is the Hunter House in Newport. When the walls of this northeast parlor were stripped during restoration, the paneling was returned to its original mellow putty color. Stripping also revealed pilasters, painted to imitate black marble, and painted cherubs over the built-in cabinet, the interior painted green to display the china.

1. Photographer: L. Barrow (Courtesy, *Life* Magazine).
2, 4. Photographer: Guerrero.
3. Photographer: Alfred T. Wyatt (Courtesy, Fairmount Park, Philadelphia. Endowed by the Estate of Naomi Wood).

2

3

4

1

2

Ours is not the only era to be enamored of pattern on pattern. In the eighteenth and even more in the nineteenth century, patterns were mixed with spendthrift bravura and style.

1. Dominating the Chinese Room at Beauport in Gloucester, Massachusetts, is a magnificent handpainted Chinese wallpaper which Henry Sleeper found in a Marblehead attic, perfect after a century of storage. Mrs. McCann, who bought Beauport after Sleeper's death, turned the room into a delightful riot of Chinese Chippendale and chinoiserie.

2. Another stunning wallpaper, depicting the adventures of the Knights of Charlemagne and printed in France in 1828, covers the walls of Rosedown's entrance hall in one glorious sweep. The original paper was duplicated, as were the border and dado. An English rug contributes yet another pattern to the hall.

3. The winter dining room at Liberty Hall, Kenansville, North Carolina, an 1880 house restored as a museum, is a skillful counterpoint of three patterns. Played off against each other are an antique Hamadan rug, striped fabric on the chair seats, and wallpaper with a bird-and-flower pattern taken from an eighteenth-century Pillement design. The fabric and wallpaper were researched for the restoration by Zelina Brunschwig, ASID, reproduced by Brunschwig & Fils.

4. The gentleman's library in the Wickham-Valentine House in Richmond, Virginia, is surprisingly up-to-date in its interplay of two strong patterns, one the Persian Heriz rug, the other the Brunschwig & Fils curtain fabric, a madder-red-and-blue print based on a stenciled and painted indienne cotton border design dating back to the 1770's.

1. (Courtesy, S.P.N.E.A.).
2. (Courtesy, McMillen Inc.).
4. Photographer: Henry S. Fullerton (Courtesy, *Antiques Magazine*).

1

2

3

Just as the fireplace was the focal point of a daytime room, so was the protectively sheltered four-poster the cynosure of the bedroom, with the bed treatment conforming to the style of the bed, or following the fashion of the time. The four-poster in the McIntire Bedroom at the Museum of Fine Arts, Boston (1), shows the master's touch in the beautifully carved posts and canopy with gilded sheaf of arrows, torchère, and urn finials. The crisply scalloped and fringed hangings, in a French commemorative toile, have a similar elegant formality.

Andrew Jackson's bed in the bedroom of his Tennessee home, The Hermitage (2) may be one of six he bought in Philadelphia in 1838. The elaborate fringed and tasseled red silk bed hangings that drape the ponderous mahogany four-poster like a sultan's tent are duplicates of the originals.

In the Landon Carter Wellford bedroom of the Valentine Museum (3), the bed treatment is in the Sheraton style, a gracefully swagged canopy caught up with fabric rosettes and lined with a solid-color fabric. The rose-printed cotton was reproduced by Brunschwig & Fils from a document of an English 1780 handloomed cotton, and the coverlet is a replica by Fieldcrest of an 1840 candlewick bed covering.

1. (Courtesy, Museum of Fine Arts, Boston).
2. (Courtesy, *Country Beautiful,* from *Great Historic Houses of America*).

3
Decorating, Then and Now

The axiom that the more things change the more they remain the same pertains as much to decorating as to any other aspect of life. The black-and-white floor or blue-and-white color scheme are as popular today as they were three centuries ago. The stenciled wall, an early artifice for capturing the look of expensive wallpaper at a nominal cost, is with us again, this time more for esthetic than for economic reasons.

Good design makes sense no matter what the era: it has a validity that can survive, even flourish on, constant updating. Who could better the rocking chair, the modular storage system (devised by those early pragmatists the Shakers), the trundle or hideaway bed, and the Venetian blind?

It is both fascinating and instructive to compare side by side the way a decorating problem was handled in the past and how it is handled now, for it clearly illustrates the underlying design principles that have withstood the test of time. Sometimes the old way even looks better and fresher than the new interpretation, which may be one reason why we have taken to reviving such early American arts as the stenciled wall and stained floor, the painted floorcloth and window shade, and the decoration of inexpensive wood furniture with false graining, marbleizing, and other *trompe l'oeil* deceptions.

In the seventeenth century, American ingenuity with paint endowed plentiful local materials with the colors and patterns of marble and expensive woods. The wood floor, copied from an early New Hampshire room, in the Murphy Room of the Bayou Bend Collection at the Houston Museum of Fine Arts (1), is a painted simulation of the black-and-white checkerboard of marble found in Dutch interiors of that time.

Today, the same motif may be used in a less traditional, more dramatic way. In a dining room (2), a checkerboard-patterned paper covers walls and ceiling, introducing a strong decorative design that makes the room look more furnished than it is.

2. Photographer: Pinto/Massey.

1

2

1. Although it hardly looks antique, the dashing blue-and-white checked fabric of the bed hangings in a room at Colonial Williamsburg is a reproduction of an eighteenth-century "tavern check," so called because it was widely used at that time in inns and taverns.

2. While checks remain perennially popular, instead of a single color we are apt to use a combination of two colors. In this bedroom-sitting room designed by Pratt Williams, the checked fabric is also distributed throughout the room and played off against the equally strong patterns of the rug and armchair.

3. The seventeenth-century checkerboard floor reappears in the family dining room of the nineteenth-century Carroll Mansion in Baltimore, this time as a floorcloth, the painted canvas summer replacement for heavy carpets in Southern homes that presaged the later invention of linoleum. (Floorcloths are again handmade today, but they are no longer inexpensive substitutes.)

4. Instead, twentieth-century technology has given us the equally decorative, but much tougher vinyl tile, manmade to resemble everything from brick and marble to, in this instance, the old-time stylized designs of the stenciled floor.

5. Painted decoration is one of the glories of the Owens-Thomas House in Savannah. In the dining room, the floor of Georgia pine planks is striped with paint to give the effect of two woods, an unpretentious treatment in striking contrast to the pale-pink walls and rich formality of the nineteenth-century furniture and elaborate cornice and curtains.

6. In today's decorating idiom, fine wood may be treated with seeming irreverence—for a good reason. The vivid red stain on the parquet floor of this bedroom designed by David Barrett, ASID, provides a zing of contemporary color that pulls together all the elements in the color scheme of black, white, and red.

1. Photographer: Guerrero.
2. Photographer: Beadle.
3. (Courtesy, The Peale Museum, Baltimore).
4. Photographer: Grigsby (Courtesy, Amtico).
5. Photographer: Helga Studios.
6. Photographer: Grigsby.

1

2

5

6

1. One of the most popular of all decorative window treatments in the eighteenth and nineteenth centuries was the shade of translucent cloth or paper, painted with stylized romantic views or primitive scenes, which, when drawn, could be seen from inside or outside the house, softly illuminated by daylight or lamplight. An antique painted shade hangs like a painting over a stairwell window in a collector's house designed by Richard Himmel, ASID.

2. Today's painted shade is more likely to resemble abstract art; witness the shades patterned with flowing shapes in black vinyl paint with which interior designer William Welsh screened out a drab and uninspiring cityscape.

3. The Austrian shade is an enduringly popular form of window dressing. In a simple eighteenth-century room in Whitehall, Newport, the silk shades control light and drafts while keeping the lines of the windows unobstructed.

4. A present-day handling of the Austrian shade in a Victorian-inspired sitting room designed by David Barrett, ASID, is actually more formal than its eighteenth-century counterpart, a combination of shade, café curtains, and ruffled and swagged overcurtains.

5. Many early decorating devices have survived the centuries unchanged because they fill a need. A case in point is the Venetian blind, which arrived here from Europe in the eighteenth century. The original Venetian blind, like the one in the parlor of the Wright-Stanly House in New Bern, North Carolina, had handmade wooden slats painted or stained to match or contrast with the walls.

6. The vertical blind of narrow shade-cloth strips is our improvement on the horizontal-slat Venetian blind. A vertical blind was used by Emily Malino, ASID, in an old-fashioned high-ceilinged ground-floor apartment to provide privacy, hide an air conditioner, and unify the window and walls—all without sacrificing natural light.

1. Photographer: Hedrich-Blessing.
2. (Courtesy, Window Shade Manufacturers Association).
3. Photographer: Guerrero.
4. (Courtesy, Celanese Corporation).
5. Photographer: Helga Studios.
6. (Courtesy, Window Shade Manufacturers Association).

52

1

3

2

5

4

6

53

Contemporary, a much misused word, is often regarded as synonymous with modern. Actually, an eighteenth-century room was as contemporary in its time as a modern room is now. While architecture, color scheme, and even furniture styles may be the same, it is how they are treated that determines whether a room belongs to the past or the present.

1. The drawing room of Mount Pleasant in Philadelphia, with its paneled and painted walls and mantel, pedimented door, fine plasterwork, and restrained color scheme of gray woodwork and pale yellow plaster, with a stronger yellow in the damask upholstery, is completely in the eighteenth-century classical tradition. The furniture, mostly of wood, with a minimum of upholstered pieces, is arranged around the walls and fireplace, and the customary Oriental rug graces the polished wood floor.

2. While the present-day living room designed by Terence Black has similar proportions and a great deal of eighteenth-century furniture, ranging from a Georgian wing chair and Chippendale ladderback armchairs to a French chest and gilt mirror, the influence of the twentieth century takes over in the color scheme, brilliant green and yellow sharpened by plenty of white, and the center-of-the-room seating group of oversized upholstered sofas flanked by sleek white-lacquered Parsons tables.

3. The Turkish corner of the 1890's, inspired by Sir Richard Burton's *Arabian Nights*, a fantasy of Oriental rugs, draperies, and motifs, and a divan voluptuously piled with pillows, was the nearest the Victorians came to admitting sex into the parlor.

4. Paradoxically, the "Swinging Seventies" version of the Turkish corner, designed by Jack Lowrance, is much more restrained in execution, although uninhibited in color and pattern. Most of the furnishings, from the inexpensive cotton bedspreads covering walls and studio beds to mirror-embroidery cushions and carved figurines are from India. A clutch of cacti adds a homegrown Southwest note.

1. Photographer: A. J. Wyatt (Courtesy, Fairmount Park, Philadelphia. Maintained by The Philadelphia Museum of Fine Art).
2. Photographer: Chuck Ashley.
3. (Courtesy, The Bettman Archive, New York).
4. Photographer: Max Eckert.

54

1

3

2

4

1. In the eighteenth century, less affluent Americans espoused stenciling as a means of imitating the fashionable but costly imported wallpapers. Even the smallest or humblest chamber, like this tiny bedroom off the kitchen of the 1780 Winslow-Crocker House in Yarmouthport, Massachusetts, was brightened with simple stylized motifs of fruit, flowers, and leaves, stenciled directly onto the plaster walls by itinerant artist-decorators.

2. The old art of stenciling has recently been revived for much the same reason—to bring colorful changeable pattern to a room at nominal cost. Rather than using carpet or tile, Paul Krauss, ASID, patterned the floor of a bedroom with an overscaled stencil design that, while in keeping with the traditional furniture, is completely modern in its eye-arresting scale and color.

3. A typical nineteenth-century treatment of the perennially popular four-poster bed in the Lady's Bedroom at Liberty Hall, the recently restored ancestral home of the Kenan family of North Carolina, plays off coral-and-white striped hangings, canopy and dust ruffle against a busily patterned Directoire documentary wallpaper. Fabrics and wallpaper are reproduced by Brunschwig & Fils.

4. For today's simpler decorating style, a 1920 machine-carved copy of the same type of bed, with canopy removed and finials added, was cut down to reduce the height and painted white. A coverlet matched to the fabric used on walls and for curtains blends the bed into the background to further minimize its scale.

1. Photographer: Richard Cheek (Courtesy, S.P.N.E.A.).
2. Photographer: Harry Hartman.
3. Photographer: Henry S. Fullerton.
4. Photographer: Ernest Silva (Courtesy, Celanese Corporation).

3

4

1

2

1. As crisply fresh as a snowfall, the austere all-white bedroom of George Washington at Mount Vernon is dominated by the size and scale of an unusually wide four-poster, centered between the windows for maximum air circulation in a Virginia summer.

2. In a modern bedroom designed by Louis Bromante, ASID, an updated version of the four-poster also takes center stage, not for coolness, but to dramatize the sculptural shape and the brilliant colors of the spread, captured in double image in the mirror-paneled wall.

3. The eighteenth-century pattern for a kitchen concentrated cooking and conversation in one room, for warmth and companionship. The brick fireplace is the hub of activity in the Tryon Palace restoration at New Bern, North Carolina.

4. Modern families still favor the one-wall cooking center, but brick is now an adornment, rather than a necessity, and the old dining and food preparation table has been replaced by a built-in plastic-topped snack counter.

1. (Courtesy, Mount Vernon Ladies Association).
2. Photographer: Robert Riggs.
3. Photographer: L. H. Frohman.
4. Photographer: Tom Yee.

3

4

1 2

1. The Shakers, nineteenth-century exponents of functionalism in furniture, devised a compact system of multiple modular storage for communal possessions or, in this room from the Shaker Village, Hancock, Massachusetts, herbs dried for sale.
2. A present-day storage system in a room designed by Richard Knapple of Bloomingdale's adopts a similar arrangement of plastic drawers and shelves, set in a flushed-out wall.
3. The home office or work room is hardly a new idea. In Victorian days, when houses were large, Governor Alexander Ramsey could have a whole room as his office.
4. Now, with space at a premium, the "office" may be no more than a steel-and-glass hunt table in the living room that switches from desk to dining table as needed.

1. Photographer: Harry Hartman.
3. (Courtesy, Minnesota Historical Society).
4. (Courtesy, Celanese Corporation).

3

4

1

3

1. In the Queen Anne dining room at Winterthur, the paneled mantel, painted the soft muted green of the eighteenth century, is enhanced by a fireplace border of English Delft tiles in a subtle color combination of amethyst and white that is matched by the colors in the chair upholstery.
2. A reproduction mantel of the same period, in a room designed by Mallory-Tillis, ASID, was updated with a deep blue glaze and modern tiles dotted with the vivid colors of the printed fabric and spatterdash floor.
3. The parlor of the Morris-Butler House in Indianapolis, with its massive chandelier suspended from an elaborate foliate ceiling, reflects the Victorian penchant for excess.
4. A ceiling of the Seventies designed by Theresa Capuana is molded not with plaster but with white nylon, stretched over a framework in undulating sculptural curves. A cone-shaped opening funnels light into the center of the room in a new version of the chandelier.

1. (Courtesy, The Henry Francis du Pont Winterthur Museum).
2. Photographer: Grigsby.
3. (Courtesy, Historic Landmarks Foundation of Indiana).
4. Photographer: Otto Maya.

2

4

63

1

1. When Colonel Robert Milligan built his house in Sarasota, New York, in 1853, the Rococo Revival was the height of fashion. In typical Victorian style, the parlor floor is muffled from wall to wall with floral pattern "Brussels carpeting," the marble fireplace is crowned by an extravagantly rococo mirror, and an ornate chandelier hangs from a ceiling embellished with plasterwork which in those days, like the metal valances, was mass-produced. The matched set of rosewood chairs and sofa was made for the Milligans by the Galusha Brothers of Troy, New York.
2, 3, 4. Switch to the 1970's and a similar nineteenth-century room, still with its marble fireplace and moldings, is otherwise stripped to the bone. Instead of being hidden by curtains, the windows have pull-up shades. The floor is bare, the only decorative objects are plants and art, and rather than a heavy lighting fixture, the ceiling has a space-expanding, painted cloud cover. Most revolutionary of all is the multi-functional furniture system designed by architect Dennis Holloway; it is composed of three tri-level plywood boxes on casters, with foam-rubber bolsters and mattresses, which can be grouped in thirty-six different ways.

1. (Courtesy, The Brooklyn Museum).
2, 3, 4. Photographer: Norman McGrath.

2

3 4

65

4

The Great American Designers

In the early eighteenth century, as America moved into a more settled era of trade, wealth, and expansion, a distinctive and indigenous style of design and decoration began to emerge, with the colonial craftsmen originating their own interpretations of the European modes. Europe has been traditionally the firm foundation on which American design rests; Jefferson drew much of his inspiration from Italy, France, and England. Samuel McIntire was strongly influenced by Adam, Duncan Phyfe by Sheraton and French Directoire. Two famous nineteenth-century cabinetmakers, Belter and Mallard, were respectively German and French. This interchange continued throughout the twentieth century. Among our leading furniture designers, Harry Bertoia came from Italy, Mies van der Rohe from Germany, Tommi Parzinger from Austria, Jens Risom from Denmark, Eero Saarinen from Finland, and T.H. Robsjohn-Gibbings from England—but it was in America that they found the fullest scope for their talents.

The strength of American design is that it has never been tradition-bound or rigidly purist, but a living, fluid, vital force in a young and innovative country quick to adopt new materials, processes, techniques, styles, and color combinations. For this we can thank the American designers who started the trends, guided taste, and envisioned new stimulating concepts of space and decoration that have made our home life richer and more fulfilling.

Designers two centuries apart are linked by their avant-garde ideas.
1. For his library-bedroom suite at Monticello, Thomas Jefferson devised a space-saving alcove bed that bridged two rooms. Also of his design is a chaise that combines a chair and padded bench and pull-over writing table for relaxed reading and writing.
2. A living room designed by Richard Ohrbach centers on a multi-purpose seating unit that splits up into a variety of groups. An Edward Fields rug reinforces the undulating stripes of the Morris Louis painting, keeping the room supercharged with color.

1. Photographer: Helga Studios (Courtesy, *Antiques Magazine*).
2. Photographer: Bill King.

1

Thomas Jefferson's Palladian-style country mansion, Monticello, is testimony of the innovative inventive mind of this first of a tradition of American architect-designers.

1. Inspired by the dome of the Hôtel de Salm in Paris, Jefferson crowned the west portico with this copy over the octagonal "sky room."

2. In the library of the bedroom suite stands Jefferson's octagonal file table with revolving top and eight drawers, inlaid alphabetically. Simple red damask swags lined with green linen, another design of Jefferson's, substitute for draperies, revealing the shape of the windows, and letting in more light.

3. A similar window treatment, in the light sheer white dimity that was mostly used for clothing at that time, does not obstruct the floorlength triple-sash window exit from the tea room to the piazza.

4. Above the door in the entrance hall, Jefferson installed a two-faced clock that can be seen from inside and outside. In addition to telling time, the clock has a system of counterweights—Revolutionary War cannonballs on cables running over pulleys. One set moves down the opposite wall, ticking off the days marked there.

Photographer: Helga Studios (Courtesy, *Antiques Magazine*).

3

4

1

Louis Comfort Tiffany, although best-known for Tiffany glass, began his career as an artist, studied in Paris, and then became an interior decorator. In 1881, Tiffany and his group, Associated Artists, designed the interiors of Mark Twain's house in Hartford, Connecticut, incorporating the new trends that were to flower into Art Nouveau. In the dining room (1), panels of Tiffany glass border the delicate tracery of the window over the fireplace, where Twain liked to watch "the flames leaping to meet the falling snowflakes." More of Tiffany's work appears in the stenciled walls of the library, shown on page 21.

Frank Lloyd Wright, the great exponent of organic architecture, followed the Jeffersonian tradition, designing lighting, heating, ventilation, and furniture for his houses. To him, they were "mere details of the character and completeness of the structure." Furniture was the least satisfactory for him. He confessed that he found it difficult "to design furniture as architecture and make it human at the same time." In the D. D. Martin House in Buffalo (2), a 1904 prototype of Wright's "prairie houses," the stark lines of Wright's barrel-back chairs and his massive sofas, with cupboards built into the arms, echo the strength of the interior architecture. Falling Water, Bear Run, Pennsylvania (3), one of Wright's most famous houses, was built in 1936, and is typically rustic and organic both in mood and materials. For the H. C. Price House in Scottsdale, Arizona (4), built in 1955, Wright designed the lighting and furniture, much of it built in.

1. (Courtesy, Mark Twain Memorial, Hartford, Connecticut).
2. Photographer: Bill Aller.
3. Photographer: Hedrich-Blessing.
4. Photographer: Maynard L. Parker (Courtesy, Previews, Inc.).

2

3

4

Elsie de Wolfe, or Lady Mendl, is usually credited as the originator of a completely American twentieth-century decorating style. Her first major commission, after opening her shop in New York in 1904, was to decorate the interior of the new Colony Club for women. "Suitability" was her battle cry. Sweeping aside precedent, she made over the dining room into a light fresh garden room with bare floors, plants, and a background of green treillage (1), which she described as "a mural decoration, architectural in treatment." (She was the first person in this country to use treillage indoor.) In the 1930's, she outmoded the old *en suite* living room, using instead a mixture of modern and period furniture, blond wood finishes, a neutral background accented with emerald green, and indirect lighting in niches (2). The animal-hide rug on wall-to-wall carpeting was one of her trademarks, like the chintz she lavished on her own bedroom in 1943, repeating the motif in paint and appliqué (3). Other distinctive touches are the painted *trompe l'oeil* ribbons and moldings, mirror panels backing the bed and on the closet door, a pair of matching night tables and lamps.

Elsie de Wolfe's highly individual style foreshadowed the modern idiom of the 1940's and 1950's, expressed in serene neutral backgrounds stressing such materials as travertine and marble, indirect lighting, solid-color carpets and upholstery, and sleekly graceful lightly-scaled contemporary furniture. Examples of the new modernism of those decades are the work of two of the day's leading designers of, and major influences on, furniture and interiors, T. H. Robsjohn-Gibbings (4), then designer for Widdicomb, and Edward Wormley (5), designer for Dunbar, whose furniture followed more architectural lines.

2. (Courtesy, *Country Life*).
4. Photographer: Lisanti (Courtesy, *House Beautiful*).
5. Photographer: Guerrero (Courtesy, *House & Garden*).

1

2

3

4

5

4

5

3

American designers today cultivate a style as personal as a signature.

A contemporary treillage room by Barbara D'Arcy, ASID, of Bloomingdale's, reveals the fresh inventive way she updates the romantic past (1). The crisp clean contemporary statement of bold color and art silhouetted against white is typical of the approach of Richard Himmel, ASID (2). The all-white room, an easy mix of crude and sleek textures, city elegance, and country simplicity (3), bears the unmistakable stamp of Michael Taylor, ASID. Intense splashes of color in woven fabrics, arresting displays of folk art against a bleached-sand background, bear the imprint of Alexander Girard (4). The easy eclectic look for which David Barrett, ASID, is famous combines a potpourri of diverse furniture, art, and objects from many countries (5).

2. Photographer: Fred Lyon.
3. Photographer: Milton Greene (Courtesy, *Life Magazine*).
4. Photographer: Idaka.
5. Photographer: Otto Maya.

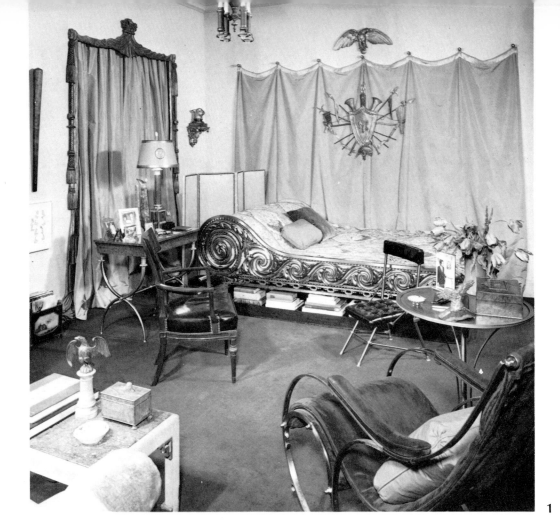

1

2

3

4

5

American interior design encompasses every style, from traditional to avant-garde.
1. A traditionalist with a flair for reinstating the glories of the past, Michael Greer, ASID, spurred the revival of antique steel furniture, like these nineteenth-century English and French pieces from his collection, some of which he reproduced.
2. Although Edward Fields, America's foremost rug designer, is best known for modern designs, he created this rug for the White House Diplomatic Reception Room.
3. One of the first interior designers to bring clashing psychedelic mixtures of color and pattern to a room was James Tillis, ASID, of Mallory-Tillis.
4. The dramatic interiors of fabric designer Jack Lenor Larsen express his lively visual imagination. In his own ever-changing apartment, arresting colors and patterns stand out against walls, reshaped with white nylon on a wooden framework.
5. The name of the late Arthur Elrod became synonymous with the Southern California style—rooms linked to outdoors, bold colors, contoured furniture.

1. Photographer: Max Eckert.
2. Photographer: Ernest Silva.
3. Photographer: Louis Reens.
4. Photographer: John T. Hill.
5. Photographer: Leland Lee.

1

Of all the influences on twentieth-century decorating, probably the most enduring has been that of a line of interior designers stretching from Elsie de Wolfe and Ruby Ross Wood to Dorothy Draper, Mrs. Archibald Brown of McMillen Inc., Melanie Kahane and William Pahlmann. They might be classified as modern traditionalists each of whom in a different way treats period furnishings with a healthy irreverence, adroitly teaming them with the colors, fabrics, and backgrounds of our day.

1. Green-and-white striped wallpaper and a floral print, often overscaled pink or red cabbage roses, was the trademark of the late Dorothy Draper. She was also one of the first interior designers to renew traditional furniture with inexpensive chintz.

2. The special forté of Mrs. Henry Parish, II, who has designed rooms for the White House, is teaming simple provincial furniture of different periods with fresh colors and mixed patterns in a sophisticated version of the Country Look.

3. The restrained opulence of William Pahlmann's traditional rooms is invariably sparked with the surprise of unexpected color—fauteuils upholstered in brilliant leather, or the touch of hot pink in this room of rich reds and mahogany.

4. The mood that Melanie Kahane sets in her traditional rooms is restful, soft, and appealing, a combination of pastels, furniture bleached or painted white, dressmaker details on upholstered furniture, and a few elegant accessories.

1. Photographer: Guerrero (Courtesy, *House & Garden*).
2. Photographer: John T. Hill (Courtesy, *Time*).
3. Photographer: Louis Reens.
4. Photographer: Grigsby.

2

3

4

1

2

3

LANDMARKS IN FURNITURE DESIGN

The fortunes and fashions of America may be traced through the progression of furniture design. When all furniture was made by hand, only the wealthy could afford to commission the services of fine cabinetmakers. Today, with furniture companies reproducing or adapting the best of the past, many of the classics of our design heritage are within the reach of the average American, and the fine points of the originals may be studied in museum collections.

1. A pair of Hepplewhite chairs, carved by Samuel McIntire around 1795, and other furniture of the same style and period, are shown in the McIntire bedroom, part of the Bayou Bend Collection of the Museum of Fine Arts, Houston.

2. Duncan Phyfe furniture in the Regency style is the jewel of this Federal dining room, with a typical drapery treatment of the time. Phyfe made the set of mahogany curule chairs for a New York merchant, who also owned the multi-colored crystal chandelier and candelabra.

3. A glorious example of Victorian Rococo, the best of the revivals, is this Belter Parlor with its intricately carved rosewood furniture. The fabric was reproduced from the original upholstery of a similar parlor set from an 1856 house near Port Royal, Virginia, and the floral-patterned Wilton carpet was found in Boston.

2, 3. (Courtesy, The Metropolitan Museum of Art, New York).

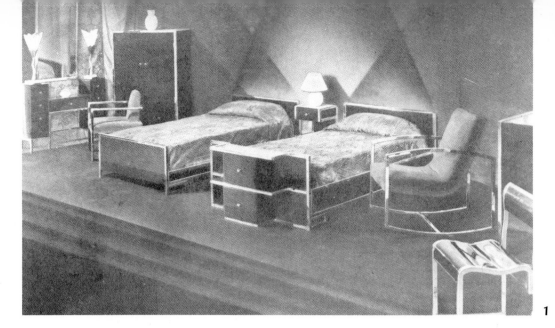

In the twentieth century, furniture came under the austere influence of the Bauhaus School, the modernism of Art Deco, and the simplicity of Scandinavian Modern. Metals became increasingly important in construction, and new pieces evolved to meet the needs of the day. This bedroom set in glossy burnished black and chrome nickel, designed in 1929 by Norman Bel Geddes (1), typifies the style now called Art Deco. In the 1940's, industrial designers like Russell Wright were the style setters. His living room furniture of maple, with the then-popular blond finish (2), reflects the changing patterns of living. The hinged-top cocktail table, lightly-scaled chairs, and modular cabinet with drop-leaf desk are designed for small rooms and limited space. The plug-in pole storage system designed by George Nelson for Herman Miller in 1958 (3), an outgrowth of his 1948 storage wall, moved storage into the open, creating a divider for the open-plan rooms of the time. Paul McCobb's light-weight off-the-floor furniture, in combinations of wood and metal or plastic (4), was designed for the young budgets and tastes of the 1950's.

2. (Courtesy, *All About Modern Decorating* by Mary Davis Gillies).
4. Photographer: Lisanti.

3

4

The vitality and variety of expression found in American contemporary furniture was greatly fostered by companies such as Knoll Associates and Herman Miller, who commissioned and produced the designs of Harry Bertoia, Mies van der Rohe, Eero Saarinen, Charles Eames, George Nelson, and Alexander Girard, and the Museum of Modern Art's 1941 "Organic Design in Home Furnishings" exhibition and subsequent Good Design Shows. This selection shows some of the outstanding designs from 1929 to the present day.

1. The simple sculptural forms of George Nakashima's furniture, which accentuates the beauty of the wood grains, recall the work of earlier American craftsmen like the Shakers.

2. The contoured wire-mesh shell chair was sculptor Harry Bertoia's unique contribution to furniture design.

3. The award-winning chairs of designer Charles Eames have been a major influence on modern furniture. From his experiments with molding laminated plywood came this 1956 lounge chair and ottoman.

4. Architect-designer Warren Platner's first entry into the realms of residential furniture in 1966 was this sculptured steel-wire collection for Knoll.

5. Probably the most famous of all contemporary classics is the X-frame steel-and-leather Barcelona chair by Mies van der Rohe, designed for the Barcelona Exposition of 1929, shown here in the equally famous glass house of architect Philip Johnson.

6. Harvey Probber has been a pioneer in the concept of modular seating with a long built-in look since the introduction of his "Nuclear" group in 1945. This "Tufto" group of molded urethane foam, covered in fabric, leather, or vinyl, is strictly Seventies.

1, 2. Photographer: Lisanti.
3. (Courtesy, Knoll International).
4, 5. Photographer: Ezra Stoller (Courtesy, Knoll International).

1

2

3

4

5

6

1

2

3

4

1. To own the pedestal-base mushroom table and tulip chairs designed by Eero Saarinen, another architect who won fame for furniture design, was a 1950's status symbol.

2. The dramatic trend-setting furniture of Milo Baughman has been part of the American scene since 1948, when he was identified with the emerging "California Modern" style.

3. The latest venture of interior designer Angelo Donghia, who also has wallpapers, fabrics, and upholstered furniture to his credit, is a line of bed linens. His windowpane check, repeated in giant scale on the floor, keynotes a bedroom in crisp natural tones.

4. The enchanting and colorful designs of artist-designer Vera, can now be found on sheets, curtains, and the bedspreads and needlepoint pillows in her bedroom.

1. Photographer: Guy Morrison.
3. (Courtesy, J. P. Stevens).

1

2

3

When the trade magazine known as *The Decorator's Digest* changed its name to *Interior Design and Decoration* in 1937, henceforth referring to the erstwhile "decorator" as an interior designer, it was in recognition of the fact that an interior was a totality of design, as Jefferson and, before him, the Adams Brothers, had been aware. Just as architects eventually designed furniture for their houses, so the expertise of furniture and interior designers gradually extended to every aspect of a room, from fabrics, wallpaper, and carpets to lighting, accessories, even china, silver, and crystal.

1. From designing interiors, Ward Bennett branched out into sleekly contemporary furniture of steel, glass, and marble, shown here in his remodeled apartment in the upper reaches of New York's famous old building, The Dakota.

2. Tommi Parzinger has been a leader in modern furniture since his arrival in the United States in 1932. His highly individual designs, rooted in the Viennese style, are elegant and timeless, with simple, graceful proportions, unusual woods, and glowing lacquer finishes. Although furniture is his love, he also designs fabrics, carpets, lighting fixtures, and accessories.

3. Vladimir Kagan, ASID, who heads his own design and furniture manufacturing firm in New York, is perhaps best known for his avant-garde multi-level seating, illuminated furniture, and tubular lighting, and for rooms such as this one, which bear his easily recognizable pace-setting touch.

1. Photographer: Jon Naar.
3. Photographer: Louis Reens.

1

2

3

4

5

Today, as in the past, architects and artists are the ones who contribute the truly explorative concepts for living. To architect Paul Rudolph, lighting and graphics are the most potent and inexpensive tools for transforming the indoor environment. The mood and character of his apartment living room (**1**), a totality of white textures, can be altered at will with colored lighting and illusory back projection (**2**).

The complexity of living in a small space in the city is a challenge that architect Gamal el Zoghby meets by constructing totally coordinated environments devoid of furniture or decoration that face the realities of living in a spirit of truth and logic. Within an existing apartment he assembled geometric units—steps, platforms, pillars, and alcoves—into a three-dimensional, civilized form of cave, specifically designed for the owner's needs. The carpeted steps and platforms (**3, 4, 5**) serve as chairs, tables, sofas, and beds, needing only the addition of personal belongings and decorative objects.

1, 2. Photographer: Louis Reens
3, 4, 5. Photographer: Harry Hartman.

91

2

3

To artist Aleksandra Kasuba, the ninety-degree angles and vertical and horizontal planes of conventional rooms are hostile to the senses. Within her Victorian brownstone apartment she has created a womblike space shelter: a cool quiet colorless labyrinth of white stretch nylon and sloping floors and platforms covered with neutral gray carpeting, and with an occasional circle of mirror. Inside her sensuous sculptural shells are the bare necessities for living.

The elevated dining area (1) has small white-topped tables that spring like mushrooms from the floor, and a carpeted bench. A "group shelter" (3), with a shaggy handwoven rug, provides seating at different levels. Other enclosures provide a circular "sleeping bower," and a writing shelter and work desk. Plants and people provide the only color. The senses are stimulated and soothed by the experience of different levels and slopes, and the play of light turning the nylon walls translucent (2).

To Ms. Kasuba space shelters are the living form of the future. They lend themselves to mass production and packaging, can be assembled in less than a month in multiple combinations to meet individual needs, and establish a peaceful core in which to escape the turmoil of the city.

Photographer: Harry Hartman.

5
Decorating With Collections

Collecting might be called the mark of an affluent society, for a tendency to accumulate personal luxuries and pleasures, whether these are regarded as a good investment, like art, or merely as an absorbing pursuit for leisure hours, comes after the necessities of life are secured. The great American collections of art and antiques amassed by the very wealthy—the Rockefellers, the du Ponts, Henry Clay Frick, and Joseph Hirschhorn are prime examples—have been passed on for the benefit of the nation, and constitute some of our lasting treasures. Then there were other collectors who, while not enormously wealthy, could afford to indulge their consuming passions and leave behind an American legacy, like Henry Sleeper with his highly personal New England château, Beauport. Many ordinary people are also collectors, and with no thought of profit or posterity, build their homes around their collections, sharing them with family and friends.

Rather than being displayed in museums, these at-home collections are integrated with the decoration, to be changed and rearranged in a way that keeps them fresh and perpetually stimulating to the eye and mind. Such simple collections have an historical precedent in the past, where things that today would fetch a high price were "in common use." Our collections may be more prized and more expensive, but we, too, regard them as being "in common use."

1. The Canton in the butler's pantry at Mount Vernon, arranged decoratively on a tier of shelves as it might be today, may be a collector's item now, but then it was referred to as "blew and white china in common use."
2. Pennsylvania Dutch toleware, displayed in a cabinet at The American Museum in Bath, was one of the greatest of the rural folk arts. The vivid color, an attempt to reproduce the lustre of Oriental lacquer (tole was also known then as "japanned" ware), was produced by colored varnishes baked to form a glossy surface.

1. Photographer: Walter H. Miller (Courtesy, Mount Vernon Ladies Association).
2. Photographer: L. Barrow (Courtesy, *Life Magazine*).

1

2

95

1

2   3

4   5

When Henry Sleeper, early twentieth-century interior designer, constructed Beauport, in Gloucester, Massachusetts, he designed the rooms around his acquisitions as a synthesis of the differing styles, moods, and periods of American life, from the days of the Pilgrim Fathers through the Revolution and the beginnings of the Republic. With an artist's eye and an architect's knowledge, he fused background and decoration in a way that was then totally new and individual.

A Gothic window of ground glass in a passage of the Octagon Room frames amethyst glassware ranging in tone from pale lavender to deep grape (1). Sleeper used windows in this way throughout the house to filter light through the glowing tones of glassware, an idea that has since been much copied. Often, he used this device as a means of making a color transition from one room to the next. In the Chapel Chamber, or Paul Revere bedroom (2), the influence is again the Gothic arch. The wallpaper is a Christopher Wren church design copied from the original on the walls of Paul Revere's House in Boston. The interior of the corner cabinet, painted dusty pink, accents the transferware. Initially, the cabinet held a collection of Paul Revere silver (3), which was given to the Boston Museum of Fine Arts. In the Pembroke Room, or Pine Kitchen (4), a reconstruction of an early New England keeping room, the simple brown earthenware used in Colonial times is ranged on the shelves of a pine sideboard. In the Octagon Room (5), a dining room inspired by a similar eight-walled room at Indian Hill, West Newbury, walls painted deep aubergine and a chair and desk of tiger maple are a subtle and sophisticated contrast to the collection of red tole.

(Courtesy, S.P.N.E.A.).

97

1

2   **3**

The New York brownstone of artist Theodoros Stamos is a fascinating counterpoint of American furniture classics and Art Nouveau glass and objects, and Mr. Stamos's own paintings, with each room a series of vignettes and compositions. In a bedroom corner (**1**), a laminated-top desk and chair by Louis Majorelle, Art Nouveau designer, combines with hanging and desk lamps and desk accessories by Tiffany. The bedroom alcove (**3**), with its three-dimensional *trompe l'oeil* mural by Alan Thielker, makes a dramatic background for an original Mies van der Rohe table, a Tiffany lamp, chairs by Wormley and Bruno Matheson, and a bed covered with an unusual and rare Indian embroidery.

In the living room (**2**), an all-white painting from Stamos's Infinity Field, "Lefkada" series is teamed with a horn chair and footstool, Tiffany floor lamps, and a Majorelle table and lamp. In another part of the room (**4**), a red painting in the same series faces a group of Belter armchairs, and an early Wormley sofa. The painting, in close-up (**5**), interacts with the colors and sinuous shapes of Tiffany candlesticks, vases, and candles.

Photographer: Otto Maya.

98

4

1

Ray Kindell began collecting country-store Americana twenty years ago, but his interest goes back to the days when his father ran a small-town pharmacy. To Mr. Kindell, this decorative memorabilia is an amusing and nostalgic record of a vanishing America.

The living room walls (1) are a well-schooled clutter of wooden cigar-store signs, sentimental Victorian paintings, a butcher's clock shaped like a giant fob watch (to expose the merchant's name, the hands were painted at 8:15), and antique canisters, some dating back to the time of King George III. The bentwood chair is early Thonet, the coffee table a Clark's spool-thread box with legs added. Around the rolltop desk (2, 3), a circa 1870 piece which is both a complete home office and a perfect spot to mass small bygones, are more genre paintings, among them a 1915 oil of Connecticut, a very early post-office sign, and some of Mr. Kindell's own watercolors. The swivel chair has a Thonet top on an Eastlake base, and the desk lights are bracket fixtures salvaged from an old house in Brooklyn, and electrified. Arranged on a shelf above the door (4) are hand-blown tincture bottles and Parke-Davis tins from Mr. Kindell's father's drugstore.

Photographer: Otto Maya.

100

2

3   4

1

2

3

4

5

1. Utensils of pewter and copper, arranged on shelves or silhouetted against white-washed walls, as they are here in the Hammon-Harwood House in Annapolis, Maryland, were the everyday artifacts of the colonial kitchen.

2. Today, the decorative shapes and subtle tone of old pewter become the focal point of a bedroom in quiet neutral colors, designed by David Barrett, ASID.

3. In Mr. and Mrs. Leonard Aronoff's 1790 Dutch Colonial house in Connecticut, furnished with collections of Early American furniture, china, and folk art, the table in the living room, a deceptive piece of dual-purpose furniture with a deep skirt that flips over to form a bench, is set with antique spongeware. The chairs are early examples of Pennsylvania folk art, and the chalkware figures on the mantelpiece are naive nineteenth-century substitutes for European porcelains.

4. A hutch in the dining room displays Union Shield transfer plates, and ironstone.

5. In the master bedroom, the handpainted bandboxes add color and pattern.

2. Photographer: David Massey.
3, 4, 5. (Courtesy, Waverly Fabrics).

103

This most intriguing collection of nineteenth-century Americana, which fills five floors of an old house in Manhattan, was started twenty-four years ago, before the vogue for this period began. In the parlor (1, 2), a superb Gothic Revival secretary by New York cabinetmaker Joseph Meeks holds a collection of American Parian ware. The walls, covered with an antique hand-printed paper, and the mirror are hung with paintings of the Academician, American Impressionist and Ashcan Schools, arranged vertically and symmetrically, as was the fashion a century ago. The large center painting of Isis Peak in the Grand Canyon by American Impressionist De Witt Parshall has a Stanford White frame and once belonged to J. P. Morgan. The curved mahogany sofa with gilded stenciling and painted inlay was made in New York around 1830, and the elaborate chandelier is one of a set made for the White House in 1852.

In the Tiffany Room (3) are Hudson River School paintings (an 1827 view of "Caaterskill Falls" by Thomas Cole hangs over the sofa), and a number of Tiffany vases and lamps. The chairs and end tables were made by Meeks, the piano stool with dolphin sides by Duncan Phyfe, and the pedestal table by Needles. The dining room (4) holds more of the Gothic Revival furniture that was the proud possession of every family of wealth in the mid-nineteenth century. Over the eccentric lines of an ebonized sofa by Roux, from an A. J. Davis drawing for the White Plains house he designed for a Mr. Lyons (hence the lion heads on the arms), is a painting by Rembrandt Peale, one of the eight members of the Peale family of painters represented in this room. The table is set with Staffordshire plates with transfer views taken from American prints, glassware made between 1830 and 1850 by the New England Glass Company, and Gothic-pattern spoons and forks.

Photographer: Helga Studios (Courtesy, *Antiques Magazine*).

104

1

2

3

4

Decoration is "subliminated" in the living room of S. I. Newhouse, Jr.'s apartment, designed by Billy Baldwin to house Mr. Newhouse's growing collection of modern art. The style is contemporary and masculine, the tones and textures natural, the paintings are played to the hilt. Behind the sofa is a red metal sculpture by John Chamberlain and, on the wall, a Jackson Pollock below a Ken Nolan. A Helen Frankenthaler fills the narrow space between the archways, and over one archway hangs a small Charles Hunman. On a white plinth is a sculpture by Leroy Lamis.

Photographer: John T. Hill (Courtesy, *Time*).

1

2

The famous Scull Pop Art collection is a subliminal artist's eyeview of life as it zeroes in on familiar forms, objects, and people. One wall in the lobby is dominated by Jasper Johns's "Flags" (1). Poised at the entrance to the living room, like a hesitant guest, is Oldenburg's paint-stiff "Shirt," and his old-fashioned stove with papier-mâché food can be glimpsed at the left. In the dining room (2), James Rosenquist's "Silver Skies," a larger-than-life, billboard-inspired fragmentation of people, cars, and the ubiquitous coke bottle contrasts with the French Provincial furniture.

1

2

3

Seated in another part of the lobby, a life-size plaster sculpture by George Segal of Henry Geldzahler, one of the Metropolitan Museum's curators, muses frozenly in front of a false housefront (1). To the left is Jasper Johns's "Target." The Oldenburg stove (2) reappears between "Flags" and a painting by Roy Indiana. In the library (3), many faces of Ethel Scull, snapped in a Times Square automatic photobooth and silk-screened on canvas by Andy Warhol, add up to an offbeat serial portrait.

107, 108. Photographer: Frank Lerner (Courtesy, *Time*).

Although the bronzes of Frederick Remington, Victorian chronicler of the American West, might seem a far cry from an Oldenburg, this was the popular art form of its day, and the bronzes are still highly prized. Remington's subjects—horses and riders, Indians, cowboys, trappers, and soldiers—were shown always in the context of realism and action. To accentuate this sense of movement, Stephen Chase of Arthur Elrod Ltd., designed a series of lighted niches to display a collection.

Photographer: Max Eckert.

6
Living with Tradition Today

In the past decade, more and more people, including young couples, have chosen traditional furniture for their homes. This is undoubtedly yet another manifestation of the interest in our American heritage and the desire to retain and revive what is most beautiful and valuable from our past.

Compared to Europe, little furniture was made in America, and antiques as a consequence are in very short supply. Fortunately, there is no shortage of excellent reproductions and adaptations of these native classics, taken from originals in the great collections of Colonial Williamsburg and other restorations, museums, and private houses, and cities like Newport and Charleston, which were famous for fine eighteenth-century craftsmanship. Reproductions, line for line copies, completely authentic in detail, sometimes even in finish and patina, are naturally more expensive than adaptations in which the scale, proportions, and interior fittings have been altered to conform to present-day requirements. Not only furniture, but also fabrics, wallpapers, bedspreads, accessories, china, glassware, and silver from different periods and parts of the country are currently being copied, so that it is perfectly possible to duplicate a period room today, should you wish to do so.

1. A traditional room of our time is appropriately furnished with reproductions from Baker's American Classics collection, among them a Queen Anne chair, Sheraton washstand turned lamp table and Georgian wing chairs, upholstered in a modern patchwork fabric in the liveliest of colors.
2. In a country dining room, furniture of different periods and finishes from the Drexel Heritage American Tour adaptations follows the eclectic spirit of today's decorating. An early pine trestle table is teamed with Windsor chairs and benches with hand-screened decoration and a Georgian cabinet in natural pine equipped with adjustable shelves for dining storage.

1. (Courtesy, *House Beautiful*). Copyright © 1973, The Hearst Publications, Inc.

1

2

111

2

1

3

OLD STURBRIDGE VILLAGE reproductions by the Kittinger Company, Biggs Division, were inspired by furniture in houses assembled in the museum village of Sturbridge, Massachusetts, a recreation of an early nineteenth-century farming community.

Furniture in the front parlor of the General Salem Towne House (1), is all of New England origin, dating between 1790 and 1810, and the wallpaper was reproduced from a document of the same era. The parlor is typical of rooms of the day, when the furniture, simplified American versions of English styles, was scaled to suit their modest proportions. Among the pieces being reproduced are the pole screen (2), which can have an insert of fabric or needlepoint, the Hepplewhite-style sofa (3), the Martha Washington chair, and the small round tilt-top table. The single poster bed of mahogany (4) is of late eighteenth-century design, and the original is in a bedroom of the house.

1. Photographer: James C. Ward.

4

112

1   2

3

4

SHAKER REPRODUCTIONS by the Shaker Workshops in Concord, Massachusetts, are derived from prototypes found in Shaker museums and private collections. Sold at the Workshops and in the Museum of Fine Arts, Boston, they come either completely finished or as disassembled kits, the way the Shakers themselves shipped their furniture from one village to another. The authenticity and quality of the workmanship, which adheres to the Shaker principles, can be seen in the multi-purpose slatback chair, variants of which were produced in all the communities, the dropleaf chest (originally a sewing chest), and a collection of objects, from cutting board to cupboard to sconce, designed to be hung on the peg-board rail, as useful a form of storage now as it was when the Shakers invented it (1). The large drop-leaf table, similar to a harvest table, the typical straight chairs with webbing seats, and the bench still qualify as functional, well-designed dining furniture (2). Perennially popular is the large, comfortable Shaker rocker (3), and the candle stand, which makes a neat end or night table—this version (4) is copied from a piece made in 1830.

113

1

2

3

4

5

WILLIAMSBURG FURNITURE REPRODUCTIONS by Kittinger are approved authentic copies of eighteenth-century antiques in the Colonial Williamsburg collection. Meticulous craftsmanship retains the grace and beauty for which this heyday of colonial design was renowned. A Queen Anne chair and table and high-backed Martha Washington chair bring a touch of traditional elegance to a modern glass-walled living room (**1**). The Queen Anne mahogany gateleg table (**2**), a copy of one in the supper room at the Governor's Palace in Colonial Williamsburg, has delicate shell and pendant carving on the knee of the cabriole legs. A Chippendale chair, with scroll carving flanking the knee (**3**), is reproduced from a set in the palace. The 1770 original of this chest of drawers, with its serpentine front, graduated drawers, and handcarved fretwork on the chamfered corners (**4**), is in the Peyton-Randolph House at Williamsburg. The Chippendale-style highboy (**5**) was copied from one in the George Wythe House, believed to have been made in New Jersey around 1760.

1. Photographer: Hedrich-Blessing (Courtesy, Colonial Williamsburg).

1

HISTORIC NEWPORT REPRODUCTIONS by Kittinger are authorized and exact copies of furniture made by such famous Rhode Island cabinetmakers as the Goddards and the Townsends in the days when Newport was a center of wealth and world trade. The parlor of the completely restored Hunter House in Newport is paneled with pine, painted to simulate expensive walnut (1). The damask-upholstered wing chair, with heavy webbed claw and ball feet and the distinctive Newport carved shell motif on the knee (2), is among the reproductions. Others are a mahogany desk-bookcase by Job Townsend (3), probably the most important labeled piece of all the Newport furniture, and a four-drawer mahogany chest (4) with Rhode Island block front, and Newport shell carving by John Townsend (5).

1. Photographer: Guerrero.

117

1

2

3 4

5 6

HISTORIC CHARLESTON REPRODUCTIONS of furnishings in, or made for, the great town houses of that captivating South Carolina city, cover the century from 1730 to 1830, when fine cabinetmakers flourished and wealthy merchants and planters imported pieces from Europe.

One of the treasures in the dining room of the Federal-period Nathaniel Russell House (1), now headquarters of the Historic Charleston Foundation, is a three-part Hepplewhite dining table, with center drop-leaf section rounded off by demilunes (6). French and Italian influences predominate in the celadon-green drawing room of the same house (2), where the windows are undraped, with fold-back shutters as protection against heat or storms. Currently reproduced are the Louis XVI armchairs, in fruitwood and upholstered or caned and with green-painted frames in the Venetian manner, and the fancy chairs in front of the windows. Mahogany triple chest (3) and breakfast table with Chippendale fret (5), from the Heyward-Washington Museum House are reproductions of pieces by master ébéniste Thomas Elfe, and important exemplars of his work. The walnut burl butler's chest, with flip top and baize-lined silver drawers (4), was taken from an English piece in the William Gibbes House. The reproductions are being made in America and other countries.

1, 2. Photographer: Louis Schwartz.

1

FEDERAL REPRODUCTIONS by Kittinger of originals in the Colonial Williamsburg collection reflect the delicacy and lightness that characterized this style from the early days of post-Revolutionary America. The original of the mahogany sideboard, with satinwood, boxwood, and ebony inlay (1), was made in South Carolina around 1800 and now stands in the Coke-Garrett House at Colonial Williamsburg. A mahogany love seat, with inlaid panels of bird's eye maple on the back crest rail (2), from an original made in Salem, Massachusetts, about 1810, is typical of the compact lightly scaled lines of Federal furniture, designed for the smaller houses of the time and so perfectly suited to modern apartments and houses. The high-backed armchair (3) is a replica of one made in New England around 1800, and the upholstery by Schumacher is similar to fabrics of the day. The Sheraton-style mahogany secretary (4), which probably originated in a Boston cabinetmaker's workshop, is an exemplar of the Federal style, delicate and graceful, with extensive inlays and eglomisé panels on the doors. The flap-top card table (5), attributed to the New York workshop of Duncan Phyfe, displays innovations of design and construction in the clover-leaf top, brass lion-paw feet, and side legs that swing to the rear to support the opened top.

2

3

4

5

2

1

3

4

AMERICAN CLASSICS by Baker, authentic reproductions of antiques in private collections, museums, and restorations, embraces the range of styles found from New England to the South from 1700 to 1830. The work of these Colonial and Federal craftsmen is distinguished by an innate simplicity and a native freedom of line, with regional differences in design, wood, and construction. A unique unusually proportioned Windsor chair (1) is from an original in a New England collection, made around 1775, and the Queen Anne chest beside it, also of New England ancestry, is fashioned, like the 1740 antique from which it was taken, of tiger maple. The japanned William and Mary highboy in the baroque style (2) is similar to one in the American Wing of New York's Metropolitan Museum. So is the captain's couch, with storage drawers in the base (3), a completely American piece that was made in China for a clipper-ship captain during the early nineteenth century. A "turkey breast" pine cupboard (4) is adapted from a 1770 Chippendale-style corner cupboard of Southern origin.

Queen Anne bonnet-top highboy with hand-carved shell motif by the great Charlestown, Massachusetts cabinetmaker, Benjamin Frothingham, is reproduced in the Statton Private Collection II.

Secretary with bonnet top and blockfront, an adaptation by Maddox of Jamestown of the John Goddard antique, has less detailed carving, and the proportions have been scaled down.

Thomas Jefferson's octagonal file table with revolving top and alphabetically inlaid drawers (shown in his library, page 68) is recreated down to the last detail by Kittinger.

CRAFTSMANSHIP, AMERICAN STYLE

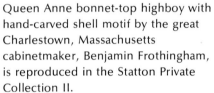

Hepplewhite-style chest made by Annapolis cabinetmaker John Shaw in 1783 for the Governor of Maryland is a reproduction from Kittinger's Old Dominion Collection.

The painted and stenciled Hitchcock chair, probably the most popular of all nineteenth-century machine-made "fancy chairs," is still being reproduced by The Hitchcock Chair Co.

123

2

3

1

124

4

5

AMERICAN TOUR by Drexel Heritage, a collection of adaptations of museum
antiques in woods appropriate to the period and with authentic detail and
decoration, encompasses the spectrum of American furniture, from country styles
to the most formal and elaborate. Curio cabinet with bonnet top (1) has been lightly
scaled for today's rooms and fitted with an interior light and adjustable shelves. The
magazine stand in oak finish (2) is a present-day adaptation of the old-fashioned
towel rack. A highboy in the Chippendale style (3) is embellished with japanned
chinoiserie decoration. The Pennsylvania dower chest in pine, with hand-screened
decoration (4), metamorphoses into a coffee or cocktail table when the sliding top
is pulled back, revealing a laminated shelf. The folding screen, with *trompe l'oeil*
panels and Pennsylvania Dutch folk-art decoration (5), is from the Et Cetera Group
of accessory pieces that complement the traditional furniture.

1

ETHAN ALLEN AMERICAN TRADITIONAL home furnishings, co-ordinated groups of furniture, fabrics, rugs, and accessories, translate the major design periods into adaptations appropriate to today's living. One example of this adaptability is the small dining room designed by Paul Krauss, ASID **(1)**. A space-stretching mirrored wall reflects a combination of styles and finishes from Hitchcock-style button-back chairs to the deep wood tones of a maple china cabinet and drop-leaf server.

Inspired by antiques in the bedroom of the 1683 Whipple House **(2)**, an historic New England landmark, the Early American Heirloom group captures the simplicity of one of the best-loved of all American furniture styles—that of the early colonies.

Rare examples of New England and Philadelphia antiques in the drawing room of The Lindens, Washington, D.C. **(3)**, were the springboard for some of the pieces in the Georgian Court group.

3

5

7

America the Colorful

A bold, uninhibited use of color and pattern is part of the American design heritage, from early folk art to current high fashion. Because of this tradition, Americans have always been quick to accept avant-garde color combinations. This tendency, allied to a perpetual parade of "Looks" initiated by interior designers and magazines, and popularized by department stores and home furnishings manufacturers, has kept decoration in a fluid state, open to the innovation or fad of the moment. Those that have lasted have validity, are pleasing to the eye, and always open to new interpretations.

Some of the all-time great looks and color schemes that have left their mark on American decorating are shown in this chapter. A few are revivals of earlier decorative styles like Art Nouveau, Art Deco, and Egyptian. Others spring from regional or national design backgrounds—the Southwest, Hawaii, the Orient, the Mediterranean. Still others are based on art and craft forms—supergraphics, psychedelic colors, patchwork—or on natural or manmade materials, from wood and wicker to mirrors and shiny vinyl.

The look of pattern on pattern has become a standard decorating device, flexible enough to be rendered in many different ways and moods.
1. For a traditional bedroom, David Eugene Bell, ASID, of Bloomingdale's, took the patchwork-quilt motif and updated this Early American look by repeating the colors of the two patchwork-printed fabrics in a strong stripe on the sofa and a polka-dot print on the chair.
2. To camouflage a brownstone's problem windows and walls, designer Natalie Schram created a bedroom that is like something out of the Arabian Nights. She took flamboyant companion patterns in curtains, readymades, and laminated shades, shirring the curtains on rods to cover the walls and using the readymades for table and cushion covers as well as for bedspreads.

2. (Courtesy, *House Beautiful*).

128

1

2

1

2

3

4

Four hardy perennials of decorating that change from decade to decade, according to the fashions of the day and the style of the designer, gaining new vitality each time, are:

1. The Great White Look of the Thirties, revamped in the Seventies by California interior designer Billy Gaylord. Soft fluid curves of the ottoman, with its three dozen puffy pillows, walls soundproofed with quilted white pocket-lining fabric (similar to elevator pads) are counterpointed by an angular coffee table of stacked whitewashed flagstones, a huge cactus, and a Zanne Hochberg plastic box sculpture.

2. Blue-and-white is a classic color scheme that defies age. Sparked with scarlet, it makes a timeless background for a bedroom by David Eugene Bell, ASID, of Bloomingdale's.

3. Black-and-white plus color is another age-old combination, revived in the Fifties by Melanie Kahane who paved a bedroom floor with black-and-white checkerboard tile, accenting it with a splash of pumpkin. In the Seventies version of designer Richard Ohrbach, the color accent on vinyl-clad walls and carpeted stairs ranges almost imperceptibly from orange to tomato to pink to violet on the landing.

4. Red, white, and blue has progressed over the years from patriotic to the Pop bedroom designed by Arthur Leaman, ASID, with its Mickey Mouse coverlet, psychedelic stretch upholstery, and glossy red plastic furniture.

1. Photographer: Chuck Ashley.
3. Photographer: Bill King.
4. Photographer: Otto Maya (Courtesy, Celanese Corporation).

3

4

The American love affair with color that began in the late Forties became ever more daring in the Fifties and Sixties, as acceptance of new and startling combinations peaked.

1. Blue and green, by far the most popular of all the Fifties color schemes, is now a decorating standby. Blue predominates in this room designed by Allan Scruggs, with emerald green scattered around solely as an accent.

2. The team of pink and orange, initiated in the early Fifties by Melanie Kahane, reappears today in a subtle rendering by Lee Bailey, where the print on the loveseats combines the colors of the walls and the rug.

3. The red-red room marked another step in the inexorable advance of color. By the Seventies, Barbara D'Arcy of Bloomingdale's could design a model room of shiny fire-engine red plastic stacking-unit furniture and storage walls, with magenta used on the sofa as an accent, without raising a suburbanite's eyebrows.

4. Clashing mixes of color and pattern were an outgrowth of the psychedelic sensory stimuli of the Sixties. This rainbow room, designed by Stephen Chase of Arthur Elrod, Ltd., takes the color mix just about as far as it can go.

1. (Courtesy, State Pavilion).
2. (Courtesy, Eastman Chemical).
4. Photographer: Max Eckert.

1   2

The back-to-earth movement of the late Sixties brought a return to natural tones and textures, not so much the subtle neutrals of the past as easy mixes of wood and rattan, fur and wool, a profusion of plants, and a range of tawny earth tones.
1. For a city version of the natural look, designer John Schaffner teamed rough, smooth, and shaggy surfaces with African art and baskets.
2. The starkly natural look found in Mediterranean houses is captured with fur and flokati rugs on tile floors, rush-seated chairs, a tiled plant shelf, and pottery and plants silhouetted against walls of thick stucco-textured paint.

1. Photographer: Ernest Silva (Courtesy, Celanese Corporation).
2. Photographer: Harry Hartman (Courtesy, *Redbook*).

135

1

2

3

4

While American decorating has always reflected strong regional influences, some looks have remained comparatively localized. Others, especially those of California, Florida, Hawaii, and the Southwest, have been adopted well beyond their own boundaries.

1. Southwest mainly in its background of pueblo-like walls and wood beams, cacti, and patterns reminiscent of Navajo rug motifs, this room by Richard Knapple of Bloomingdale's proves how smoothly the style absorbs modern furniture.

2. The California style of casual yet luxurious indoor-outdoor living is exemplified by a living room designed by Geri Cavanaugh. Backgrounds are cool, bare, and predominantly white, surfaces easy to maintain, seating king-sized and comfortable, and colors as vivid as bougainvillea, but kept to an undistracting minimum.

3. Hawaii, America-in-the-Pacific, has generated perhaps the most natural and low-keyed of all the regional looks, a blend of Oriental understatement and tropical ease. The merging of many Pacific cultures is evident in the Japanese shoji, the straight line of Chinese household furniture adopted for the oversized square bed, a contemporary version of the Hawaiian hikie, and Thai silk pillows, the only color notes in a room of pale neutrals designed to flow like water into the landscape.

4. In a totally different mood, the casual look of Florida, with its flowered chintz and rattan furniture, never dates, but remains as valid today as when this room was decorated, more than thirty years ago.

2. Photographer: Max Eckert.
3. Photographer: Guerrero.
4. (Courtesy, New York Public Library Picture Collection).

Revivals are as much a part of the American decorating scene as they are of the theatre.

1. Art Deco, the jazz-age style which popularized plastics, shiny materials, and mass-produced modern furniture, surfaces again in this living-platform designed by Barbara D'Arcy of Bloomingdale's. Undulating curves of plexiglass accentuated by colored lights, movie-house fashion, and molded plastic furniture with a hard-bumper center ring are 1970 equivalents of the embryo modern look.

2. The vintage Thirties, the golden age of Hollywood movie queens Harlow and Lombard, stages a comeback in a bedroom designed by Lee Bailey. Where the bedcover would have been real fur, now it is a fake, an acrylic pile fabric. Other shades of the Thirties are the piled-up pillows and an Art Deco wallpaper in pastel pink, blue, and lavender.

3. Art Nouveau, the turn-of-the-century predecessor of Art Deco, was the rage revival of the Sixties, cropping up in everything, from reproduction Tiffany lamps to fabric and wallpaper designs. Some of the many elements that characterize the style are assembled in this living room, with its swirling-pattern wallpaper and table cover, pierced brass lamp, shell-framed pictures, Eastern carved teak tables, tulip lighting fixtures, Victorian oak rocker, and hand-knitted throws.

4. Oriental is a style that admits of many interpretations. In this current appearance it means a fireplace wall-covering of shiny vinyl in Chinese lacquer red, backing Oriental porcelains, modern Hong Kong wicker, a Japanese Akari lantern, and a cluster of small Oriental accessories on Chinese-style coffee tables.

5. The Country Look, an equally variable and constant revival, may range from Early American to French Provincial to Portuguese. This time around it is an international mélange of hand-hewn beams, vinyl copy of a spatter-dash floor, American Windsor chairs, a painted European armoire, and a worldwide round-up of cookware.

2. (Courtesy, Eastman Chemical).
3, 4. Photographer: Harry Hartman (Courtesy, *Redbook*).
5. Photographer: Milton Greene (Courtesy, *Life Magazine*).

3

4

5

140

The ability to borrow decorating themes from other eras and cultures and adapt them freely to modern living is particularly American.
1. The ever-popular "Mediterranean Look" is basically a distillation of the styles of Spain, Italy, Portugal, Greece, and North Africa, expressed in many ways. In this California dining room by Cardan Interiors, the style is in the tradition of Colonial Spain, heavy carved furniture teamed with Mexican rugs, pottery, and tile.
2. Victorian clutter, back in fashion, is at its best when parlayed into a high-camp interior by collector-designer Joan Morse.
3. The back-to-the-womblike cave, a nostalgic recreation of the Sixties, is formed from a manmade material—urethane foam—which designer Pierre Maffroid sprayed on the walls and painted to simulate the sculptural contours of the natural rock.
4. The Egyptian influence, beloved of the French Empire, reappears in a more restrained manner in a contemporary living room by Jane Victor, ASID. Stylized hieroglyphs, taken from Tutankhamen's tomb, some woven into the rug border, others painted in relief on sliding wall panels, combine with Empire urn lamps, antique benches, and a modern steel chair with the classic X base.

1. Photographer: Max Eckert.
2. Photographer: Milton Greene (Courtesy, *Life Magazine*).
3. Photographer: Harry Hartman (Courtesy, *Cosmopolitan*).
4. Photographer: Hans Van Nes.

The dazzlingly dramatic decoration of the Sixties drew on many current sources, from popular art forms and discothèque backgrounds and lighting to the light-reflecting surfaces of mirrors, metals, and silver-foil wallpapers.

1. Supergraphic in paint slashes across the walls and floor of a white bedroom designed by John Schaffner to focus attention on the bed.

2. Chinoiserie in the Sixties moved from the decorative style of the eighteenth century into the realm of contemporary chic. In a dining room designed by Louis Bromante, ASID, the delicate tracery of treillage wallpaper and chairs with Chinese Chippendale fret backs team with the high shine of sleek white lacquer and white porcelain figures.

3. Mirrored walls and tabletops that break up color like a kaleidoscope bring an element of sparkle and constant change to a room designed by David Ramey of Birns Interiors.

4. Silvery metallic surfaces of satin-brushed chrome furniture and a foil wall covering serve to enlighten and enliven a shades-of-grey room by Barbara D'Arcy of Bloomingdale's.

1. Photographer: Ernest Silva (Courtesy, Celanese Corporation).
2. Photographer: Robert Riggs.
3. Photographer: Max Eckert.

3

4

8

All-American Rooms

Certain twentieth-century rooms bear an unmistakable "made in America" stamp—the kitchen, the bathroom, the family room, the child's room, and the garden room. Nowhere else does our age of technology, mass manufacture, manmade materials, and test-tube colors register with such a strong, sure, visual impact.

It is well-known that we spend more money on kitchens and bathrooms than on any other room in the house, and sociologists might well see this as indicative of our national character. In the pioneer days, the kitchen was the heart of the home, where the woman reigned. Compared to the upper and middle-class European households, the domestic-servant era in America was relatively brief. It was almost with a sense of relief that the American woman, after wartime upheavals, regained control of the kitchen in the Forties and began to make it once more her domain, lavishing on it every new convenience and color. The bathroom might be regarded as an alliance of two contradictory elements in our character—the dedicated pursuit of hygiene and health and a subconscious desire for sensuous, even sybaritic, luxuries and comforts. The family room and the child's room are expressions of the closeness of family life and activities, and the belief that youth is a desirable state to be fostered and indulged. The garden room is a natural extension of our love of the outdoors, not so much as a place to visit or play in, but as a place to live in and become one with.

The first all-American room was the keeping room of colonial days, so called because the fire was always kept burning. Here the women cooked, the children played, family and friends gathered for warmth, food, and companionship. In this reconstruction of an old-time keeping room in the Philadelphia Museum of Fine Arts are such typical early furnishings as a tavern table, hoopback Windsor armchair, Welsh dresser, Betty lamp, iron trivet, and three-legged iron spider, or frying pan. Today, the role of the keeping room has become divided between the kitchen and the family room.

Photographer: Lisanti (Courtesy, *Good Housekeeping*).

More than any other part of the house, the kitchen is the room where American technology and individuality meet and merge in a harmonious partnership.

1. This California living-kitchen designed by its owner, American Indian artist Ron Robles, is a sunlit place of plants and pottery, sky views, and natural textures. The stone wall beneath a narrow skylight is a kitchen garden, with herbs and house plants rooted in the earth between this and the retaining wall. For dining, early Grand Rapids country chairs surround a bulbous-legged Victorian table. The buffet, once Mr. Robles's high-school art supply cabinet, was refinished by him, and then inlaid with strips of pine and redwood.

2. A totally different living-kitchen on the East Coast combines modern equipment with a dining and home-office area furnished in New England style, with painted captain's chairs, trestle table, and an adaptation of a rolltop desk.

3. Colorful kitchens come in all shapes, sizes, and materials. Here ceramic tile, striped on countertops, plain on walls, herringbone-patterned on the floor, teams with colored and white equipment and cabinets for a kitchen that is the last word in functionalism.

4. Even a typical New York apartment galley kitchen, with its stereotyped line-up of cabinets and equipment, can achieve personality through color and pattern. Here designer Ronald Bricke painted the wall with a checkerboard design and added a vivid accent rug to the floor. A work-cum-serving cart rolls on casters between kitchen and living room-dining area.

1. Photographer: Max Eckert.
2. Photographer: Tom Yee (Courtesy, Ethan Allen).
3. Photographer: Otto Storch (Courtesy, Tile Council of America).
4. Photographer: Harry Hartman.

146

3

4

3

The one-wall cooking center was a concept born of necessity, in the days when the only source of heat was the fireplace. This 1752 kitchen in the restoration of Pottsgrove, Pennsylvania (1), with its enormous crane to hold heavy iron pots, was the forerunner of the cooking wall in a living kitchen (2) designed by Poppy Wolfe, ASID. Here the unbroken line-up of work space, storage, cooktop, oven, dishwasher, and sink is also dictated by practicality—the wall location of utility and plumbing lines. Moving away from the wall to the center of the room, in an avant-garde kitchen designed by Evelyn Jablow (3), the cooking equipment is contained in one octagonal unit, with lighting focused from a central pole.

1. (Courtesy, Pottsgrove).
2. Photographer: Louis Reens.

1

Although it might seem that the family room is an American institution that has always been with us, the room did not actually surface until the late Forties and early Fifties, when an upsurge of at-home activities (amateur movies, TV, hi-fi, and stereo, games, teen-age parties, and indoor barbecues), and a trend to more casual living and entertaining made it almost obligatory to have a room other than the living room that could be used by the entire family and their friends.

1. Ancestor to the modern family room is the rugged colonial Pine Room in the William Corbit House in Odessa, Delaware. With its brick fireplace, whitewashed and paneled walls, gate-leg table, wood settle, and comfortable Windsor chairs, this room in its day withstood much daily wear and tear.

2. In this handsome, even elegant family room designed by Leif Pedersen, ASID, the huge table alternates for dining or for workspace for someone who needs both an office at home and room for a hobby, bookbinding. Open storage shelves of laminated plastic hold files, supplies, decorative objects, and books.

3. A rather more homey family room in a remodeled basement, designed by Edmund Motyka, ASID, integrates Early American pine bunk beds and captain's chairs with a thoroughly contemporary, colorful setting. One bed, separated from its mate and covered with yellow plastic fiber, acts as a sofa. The synthetic carpet is woven in dirt-masking tones of brown and black.

4. For another family room, a conversion of an old sun porch, the existing wicker furniture was salvaged and sprayed white by designer Everett Brown, FASID, and neatly worked into the red, black, and white color scheme. In a fairly small space, Brown provided for every aspect of family entertaining, from TV, stereo, card-playing, dining and drinking to home-movie viewing. The screen is a section of the white-painted wall, contained within a frame like a constantly changing, picture.

1. Photographer: Guerrero (Courtesy, Henry Francis du Pont Winterthur Museum).
2. Photographer: Hans Van Nes.
3. (Courtesy, Heywood-Wakefield Co.).
4. Photographer: Grigsby.

4

1

3

The luxurious bathroom was a comparative latecomer in America, perhaps due to a latent lingering Puritanism that decried the indulgences of the flesh. Until the middle of the nineteenth century only a few wealthy families could revel in a fully equipped bathroom. The late nineteenth century, the age of the Moguls, when Renaissance palaces and pleasure grounds flourished on the eastern shores, saw the birth of the sumptuous highly decorative American bathroom.

1. This rendering of an 1890's bathroom, from the New York Public Library Picture Collection, is certainly in the *grande luxe* category, with its stained-glass windows, wallpaper, wood paneling, elaborate faucets, radiator, towel rail, gaslight, and a floor that might have been marble, or a recent innovation—linoleum.

2. A direct descendant, remodeled by Cardan Interiors to look antique but not old-fashioned, has a sink enclosed in an almost identical paneled cabinet, electrified oil-lamp sconces, a Victorian hat stand turned towel holder and such amusingly "sportive" touches as a spittoon and a horse feeder to organize magazines.

3. Essentially sybaritic (although the modern term is "personal care"), this bathroom designed by William McNutt for a male health buff has everything from a built-in sauna and whirlpool bath to an exercise cycle.

4. The feminine version of the sybaritic bath, movie-star style, designed for singer Dionne Warwick by Cele Pollock and Joan Schindler, is mirrored, carpeted, with a sunken tub that affords an eye-level view of an enclosed garden.

2, 3 and **4.** Photographer: Max Eckert.

153

2   3

4

Color and pattern made the next major change in the bathroom.

In a large luxurious bathroom designed by Leif Pedersen, ASID (1), a wholesale use of co-ordinated wallpaper and fabric brings decorative pattern to the chilly expanses of marble. Color was the regenerator in a bathroom with old fixtures (2). The tub base was painted a snappy purple, the floor covered with raspberry carpeting, the walls and ceiling with vinyl. Colored fixtures, like those in the bathroom designed by Helen Franklin (3), date back to the Thirties, when ceramic tile was also in fashion. All that was needed to update this bathroom was a coat of deep-blue paint. The ultimate in Seventies bathrooms (4) glitters with lights, see-through furniture, a Mylar-mirrored wall; the final touch is a hot-lips pillow.

1. Photographer: Hans Van Nes.
2. (Courtesy, General Tire & Rubber Co.).
3. Photographer: Max Eckert.
4. Photographer: Harry Hartman (Courtesy, *Cosmopolitan*).

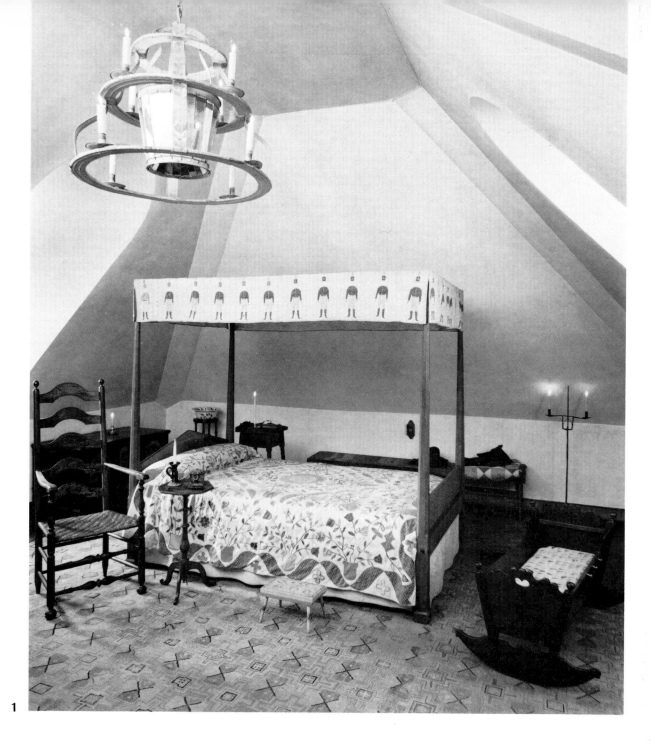

1

Children's bedrooms in the eighteenth century were not much different from those of adults. The only concessions to tender age and diminutive size in this Lebanon Bedroom at the Henry Francis du Pont Winterthur Museum (1) are the pencil-post bed valance, quilted and appliquéd with toy soldiers, and the painted yellow footstool that helped to boost a child into bed. There could be no more complete contrast than this bedroom-playroom for pampered twentieth-century twin boys designed by Jane Victor, ASID (2). Orange lacquer bunk beds, built into an existing closet, are reached by a ladder with rungs painted orange, blue, and white, the color scheme of the room. The vinyl floor is a great surface for racing cars and the lighting, custom-designed to follow the angles of the flooring, provides an even out-of-harm's way illumination for everything from rough-and-tumble games to reading or study.

2. Photographer: Hans Van Nes.

156

1

2

3

4

The room of the American child, at every age and stage from tot to teenager, is a private world, designed to accommodate the small occupant's individual interests and activities.

1. An easy-upkeep nursery in glowing sun colors, equally appropriate for boy or girl, was planned by designer Carl Fuchs to grow up with the child, after the crib has been replaced by a junior bed. The hardy cotton and synthetic plaid fabric of the spread was also applied to the floor, with several coats of polyurethane to give a diamond-hard finish. A co-ordinated stripe appears on the laminated shades, the screen, and on the built-ins.

2. Red-white-and-blue bedroom for a small boy with nautical yearnings is kept shipshape with a painted bentwood hat stand for hang-up storage, a bed with a boat-shaped plywood frame that tucks a toy chest in the bow.

3. Play corner of a bedroom for two little girls was designed by Jane Victor, ASID, as a rainbow of color in practical easy-to-clean materials, from blow-up chairs and plastic-topped table to washable vinyl wall covering, laminated shade, and cotton rug.

4. The teenage princess luxuriates in a bedroom designed by Jane Victor, ASID, that boasts a Polish bed, candy-striped curtains, and a three-way mirror between clothes closets.

1. (Courtesy, Window Shade Manufacturers Association).
2. (Courtesy, Celanese Corporation).
3, 4. Photographer: Hans Van Nes.

159

1

2

3

4

Although the outdoor or garden room had its roots in the European solarium and palm court, with our favorable climate and more casual mode of life, it evolved into something different in style and is uniquely American.
1. In 1928, the Palm Room in the Claude Boettcher Mansion in Denver still showed the influence of the old-time, year-round, formal solarium. Adrift on a sea of white marble, tropical palms in Grecian urns mingle with a Waterford chandelier, a piano lacquered white, furniture upholstered in white silk, linen, and leather, and Art Deco mirrored tables.
2. A garden family room overlooking the waters of a Long Island inlet is described by designer Anthony Hail, ASID, as "a modern evocation of an Edwardian winter room." Practical both in materials and purpose, it has a slate floor that can be mopped, tabletops made from ship's hatches, virtually indestructible, and simple wicker chairs with rugged burlap upholstery.
3. The poolside pavilion removed from the house is often found in the warmer states. With latticed walls and casual furniture, this pavilion designed by John Astin Perkins, AIA, has the aspect of a garden room, but is also equipped with dressing rooms and kitchen for entertaining.
4. The ultimate outdoor room might well be this prefab beach house in California, a big open space that becomes one with nature, as the living room opens to a deck that stretches, in turn, to the sand dunes and beach beyond.

1. Photographer: James Milmoc (Courtesy, The State Historical Society of Colorado).
2, 3. Photographer: Max Eckert.
4. Photographer: Chuck Ashley.

1

1. While the location of this garden room designed by William Pahlmann, FASID, is in the northeast zone, New York State, the plants know no season. In winter, companionably clustered on white gravel and tile platforms in front of a floor-to-ceiling wall of insulated glass, they stay healthy and flourishing, thanks to solar heat and light. In summer, louvered windows open up to let in the cooling breezes. The floor of polished brick is easily swept clean or mopped up, should water be spilled.

2. This garden room designed by Norman McD. Foster, ASID, for the hotter and more humid atmosphere of Texas, is really a lanai, in the Hawaiian tradition. It may be opened up or closed off with shutters as the weather dictates, and the ceramic-tile floor merely needs hosing down. Nothing is permanent. The light leisure furniture and plants in pots and hanging baskets can be moved indoors at a moment's notice.

1. Photographer: Alexandre Georges.
2. Photographer: Tom Leonard.

9
Updating the Antique

Even as the scientists and sociologists exhort us to prepare for a new planetary civilization where we may be living in "arcologies," rather than in our familiar cities and towns, people themselves are turning back to the past, to the traditional forms of architecture. For every family resigned to the depersonalized slot of the urban high-rise, there are many more who yearn for a farm or an old house of any vintage to restore and remake to fit their own needs.

There are, of course, practical as well as emotional reasons for buying an old property. Invariably it offers more for the money, in terms of sound construction, space, and interior charm or possibilities, than a house built today from scratch. Furthermore, in cities where Urban Renewal or Historic Restoration groups are striving to revive rundown neighborhoods, there are the advantages of tax abatement, bigger or easier loans, and financing. This doesn't explain, though, the motivation of those who build new houses to look like old ones, or who furnish a glass-walled contemporary house with antiques. This can only be due to the fact that our traditions and roots, those essential links to our past and pride of heritage, are being valued and cherished today as never before.

Home was once to many Americans a log cabin in a forest clearing. Today, privacy and an urge to get back to nature are the reasons Americans are once more taking to the woods. A twentieth-century improvement on the crude cabin or thatched hut is the geodesic dome, a simple though more sophisticated dwelling. This house, designed by Lant Realty Associates (1), and constructed of 2 x 4 struts and plywood, has much to recommend it. While snug and weathertight, it is free and open to the surrounding countryside, flooded with constantly changing light as the sun and moon rotate around the spokes of the large hexagonal window (2). The dome, thirty-eight feet in diameter, and roomier than it appears, has a second bedroom floor reached by an iron staircase (3).

Photographer: John T. Grant.

164

1

2

3

165

Many people who love the grace and charm of the past are also indissolubly wedded to the comfort and practicality of the present. When designer Pratt Williams Swanke and her architect-husband remodeled their 1882 town house in Savannah, Georgia, they contrived to have the best of both worlds. As the house was purchased from the Historic Savannah Foundation, the exterior (1) had to remain unchanged, but inside they could do as they pleased. The first major change was to transform a rear courtyard into a greenhouse (2) that, opening off the old dining room, now provides them with a dining-sitting-garden room, all comfortably air-conditioned to be enjoyed even in the heat of a Southern summer. The floor is of a practical material, dark aubergine flagstone, the furniture cool white, sparked only by needlepoint pillows—Mrs. Swanke's hobby—and a primitive landscape that glows against a mirrored wall (3).

Upstairs, three rooms on the one-time "parlor" floor became two. A couple of rooms were opened up into a sweeping living room (4) that still retains its characteristic Southern columns, arched window, and two fireplaces. Sunshine-yellow walls and white trim accentuate the beauty of the architectural detail, and the dark polished floor of imbuia, a Brazilian hardwood, is left bare, except for Oriental and leopard accent rugs. The old back parlor is now a cosy bar-cum-library-cum-music-center (5), linked by color scheme to the adjoining living room.

Photographer: Tom Yee.

166

3

4

5

1

2

168

Rescuing an historic house from oblivion can be a rewarding, if costly, endeavor. The Dr. David Ross House, built in 1749 and razed in 1957 to make way for highway construction, was discovered by its present owner as a pile of doors, windows, flooring, paneling, and 22,000 bricks in the wrecker's garage. It was painstakingly rebuilt and restored on a site in Maryland. At the time of the reconstruction, a new porch and kitchen wing were added, carefully built of old materials to match the original house (1). In the old part, the living room (2) has regained its paneling and fireplace, painted the soft green of the period, and is furnished with eighteenth-century antiques, mostly Queen Anne. In the new kitchen and breakfast room (3), a brick floor, beamed ceiling, and New England Windsor chairs capture the spirit and style of the old kitchen (4), now used as a winter party room where birds are roasted on the fireplace spit, bread baked in the brick oven. The dining room (5) also has the original paneling, and Queen Anne chairs with "kissing parrot" backs.

Photographer: Duane Suter (Courtesy, Previews Inc.)

169

Today, anyone who craves but can't afford the dignity and beauty of an old traditional house can still manage to realize that dream—or a reasonable facsimile. One answer is the colonial-style house created by Scholz Homes (1), which comes in prefabricated panels and can be assembled in any part of the country. While the house presents a traditional front, it becomes modern at the back, with a big brick patio for outdoor living and entertaining (2) that leads into a glass-walled garden room (3). The garden room is decorated, like the rest of the house, with an easy mixture of modern furnishings and traditional adaptations, both by Ethan Allen. Designed for family activities and minimum care, the garden room has a composition brick floor and walls of hardboard paneling with the look of weathered cedar planks. In the master bedroom (4), the flower-splashed fabric on walls and at windows, repeated on the canopy of the four-poster bed, introduces the ambiance of an old-fashioned garden. The dining room (5) is a study in traditional warmth, from the beamed ceiling and cherry-red carpet to the comfortable hand-decorated Hitchcock dining chairs. Comfort is also the keynote of the living room (6), with its deeply tufted tuxedo sofas in leather-like vinyl, and capacious inviting armchairs.

Photographer: Tom Yee.

170

4

5

6

This contemporary house rising from the piny barrens of Long Island (1) was inspired by the American barn. However, as the owner wanted a new, rather than a traditional house, chunks of the cedar-shingle walls were cut away and filled in with expanses of glass that open to decks on three sides, each strategically located to profit from sun, shade, and protected wind pockets. Indoors, walls and ceiling of random-width, stained cedar are an unobtrusive background for a collection of modern art started in 1958, antiques and casual, comfortable modern furniture. Art dominates a guest bedroom (2)—lithographs, Frasconi woodcuts, an early Nick Krushnik gouache and, under it, a Giacometti box turned art object. In the study (3), a Pop Art plaster shoe stands on a table, an English pub table serves as a desk. In the living room (3, 4, also shown in color on page 7), the coffee table is a caned Thonet bench topped with glass, and the floor is patterned with nomadic Arabic rugs, the geometric designs of which relate to the art collection.

Photographer: David Massey.

4

5

Nothing could have looked less promising than this century-old potato farmer's house on Long Island (1), but relieved of the sagging porch, freshly painted, and with the interior magically transformed with color, fabric, and inexpensive furniture, it began a new life as the trendiest of Aquarian-age dwellings, all the more effective for the unexpected shock value of the interior.

In the master bedroom (2), the old ceiling was ripped out to expose the roof beams. These, like the new ceiling and bedhead wall, were sheathed in star-spangled Tastemaker sheets designed by Peter Max, with matching Roman shades to mask the old-fashioned windows. The other three walls are painted, and the shimmering nightstands and bed platform are simply plywood sections covered with sheets of tiny mirrored squares. A small guest room (3) was also stripped to the bone and reclad with another Peter Max sheet pattern. Rafters and 2 x 2 framing that simulates studding, painted crisp white like the brick chimney, furniture, and cast-iron stove, break up the expanse of pattern. The headboard, also sprayed white, is a fantasy of real shells and shell macaroni.

In the master bathroom (5), the designer used more Peter Max sheets, custom-laminated, to line the tub area, and covered the ceiling with co-ordinated towels. In the tiny guest bathroom (4), more Peter Max towels, framed under glass like Pop Art prints, introduce a note of color and pattern, and to visually enlarge the room, the mirror is continued on the ceiling, outlined with theatrical strip lighting.

174

1

2

3

4

5

6

The fanciful charms of an 1890 Steamboat Gothic house in the Old Quarter of New Orleans, originally servant's quarters (1), took on a twentieth-century character when the interior was pared to the structural bones, leaving only the outer shell of the old fantastic wooden architecture. In the living room (2), the ceiling was opened to the roofline, exposing the rafters, and skylights added to flood the room with sun. Floor and fireplace wall were stripped down and painted white like the walls, and the windows were left bare, except for the architectural simplicity of louvered shutters. Sparely furnished with a modern sofa and coffee table, a few pieces of sculpture, and a 1900's Grand Rapids settee and rocker with spindly see-through shapes, the room waits like an empty stage for the color and movement of people.

By closing in and incorporating part of the porch, the new kitchen (3) was virtually doubled in size. To gain space for a master bedroom and bath (4), architect Ronald Katz created another floor under the porch, at ground level, opening up the rooms with windows and lattice screens, and creating a long linking corridor by installing broad panes of glass between the brick pillars that support the house. Because of the wholesale use of white and the limited use of furniture, this tiny house has gained a feeling of light and space that makes it seem larger than it actually is.

(Courtesy, *Life Magazine*).

2

3 4

To update a vintage 1910 Grand Rapids house
(1) that is comfortably roomy, but has no
architectural advantages, presents quite a
challenge, especially on a shoestring budget.
Interior designer Carl Fuchs left the house
much as it was, outside and in, choosing
instead to make it over by an imaginative and
thrifty use of color and fabric that also helped
to offset the heavy proportions of the
old-fashioned furniture. In the living room
overlooking the enclosed front porch (2), the
coffee table is a Victorian piece cut down,
stripped, and lightened with a blond finish.
An old dresser top, now married to piano
legs, stands between the windows. The end
table first served as a drawer file for legal
documents.

Upstairs, color converts the boxy bedrooms
into attractive retreats. Windows in the guest
room (3), painted to match the picture rail,
were given Kelly green shades. The bed is
covered with a brilliant washable Arnel
velour. An old-fashioned, hospital-type table
swings across for breakfast or reading. In the
master bedroom (5), the rounded Victorian
bay window, painted white to contrast with
the beach plum of the high-gloss walls,
accommodates another Victorian relic, a
doctor's office chaise, gaily upholstered and
piled with pillows. The white room-darkening
shades are stenciled, like the painted and
shellacked floor, and the pulls are real scallop
shells.

On the first floor, the bay becomes a
kitchen breakfast nook (4), papered and
painted in lettuce-green and white, with
pull-down and bottom-up shades for light
control and privacy. Pieces of found
furniture, like the bentwood chairs and
wrought-iron table base, now fitted with a
new wood top, are painted white. Other
finds incorporated into the kitchen are a
small bamboo display case, and an iron-based
chopping block salvaged from a butcher
shop.

Photographer: Ernest Silva (Courtesy, Window Shade
Manufacturers Association).

178

1

2

3

4

5

1

2

Nestled in a wooded Vermont hillside, this contemporary house (1) was conceived by the owner and designer, Elizabeth Dollard, as a flow of light-filled interior spaces that would provide a pure, uncompetitive background for plants and her collection of art and beautiful country antiques. Plants flourish in the garden room (2), where the floor is green Vermont slate, one of the native materials used throughout the house.

The atrium-dining room (3), and the living room directly below it (4), are planned and lighted like galleries for a movable display of paintings and art objects, like the Japanese figure and contemporary painting by a Vermont student on the eighteenth-century French sandstone mantel in the living room. Around the tiger maple dropleaf dining table are early nineteenth-century chairs, part of a set of nine. The master bedroom (5), with its bare floor of wide hand-pegged Vermont birch boards, is dominated by a graceful eighteenth-century Vermont mahogany tester bed with fishnet canopy and white-on-white crewel spread.

Photographer: Ine Wijtvliet.

3

4

5

GLOSSARY
The ABC's of Americana

In the American decorating vernacular, words and terms were added to the existing English definitions to describe those things that were unique to this country. Thus a piece of furniture might be named for a famous person, like the Martha Washington chair and table, Governor Winthrop desk, or Lincoln rocker. In other cases, it was the place of origin or the manufacturer that provided the descriptive name—for example, the Connecticut chest, Hitchcock chair, Sandwich and Tiffany glass. Pieces designed for a specific purpose, like the captain's chair, Cape Cod lighter, and the sugar chest of the South, also bore a significant name. In the twentieth century, our decorating idiom is still being expanded by additions, such as the Parsons table, the Eames chair, Pop Art and Art Deco, the "modern" style that, more than any other, might be called America's most individualistic contemporary contribution to art, architecture, and decoration. The words and terms in this glossary have a definite relationship to the American decorating scene, both past and present.

A

Acorn clock. One of the many nineteenth-century Connecticut shelf clocks which, like the banjo clock, was named for its fanciful shape.

Adaptation. A change or modification in furniture design to conform to current needs and conditions (see pages 111 and 125). An example would be a double or triple dresser in the style of an earlier single commode.

Affleck, Thomas. A London cabinetmaker who came to Philadelphia in 1763, where he produced furniture in the Chippendale style.

Amelung, John Frederick. Eighteenth-century American glassmaker and founder, in 1784, of the New Bremen Glass Manufactory in Maryland. Second only to Henry William Stiegel in fame. Amelung's factory was noted for fine copper-wheel engraving on all kinds of table glass from wine glasses and

decanters to mugs and tumblers, now regarded as of museum quality.

Americana. Furniture, objets d'art, books, and papers having to do with America, its people, and its history.

American Colonial. Generic term for furniture produced in America before the Revolution. It may be roughly divided into Early Colonial (1620–1670) and Late Colonial (1700–1790). The early pioneer style reflected the Jacobean and Elizabethan styles, adapted in crude but serviceable versions by the New England settlers, who used woods like pine, oak, and maple, mostly unfinished. Necessity, rather than fashion, prescribed the types of furniture: unadorned storage chests and cupboards; simple trestle and gate-leg tables; banister-back and ladder-back chairs with solid wood, rush, or leather seats. In Pennsylvania, German and Swiss colonists painted and decorated pieces in what we call the Pennsylvania Dutch style. The Spanish left

AMERICAN COLONIAL furniture blends harmoniously with a modern sofa, upholstered in a fabric with stylized pineapple and woodcut design, in the living room of Mr. and Mrs. Leonard Aronoff's Dutch Colonial house (also shown on page 103). The unusual comb-back rocker, a relative of the Windsor chair, dates back to 1770, and the primitive bench, adopted as a coffee table, is one of the earliest types to be used in the colonies.

(Courtesy, Waverly Fabrics).

their mark in the Mission and Ranch styles of California and the Southwest.

As the colonies prospered in the eighteenth century, more craftsmen arrived from England, bringing with them later, more elegant styles, which were promptly copied locally but simplified and changed in proportion and scale to suit New World tastes and living. By 1750, distinct American styles of furniture were being made in walnut and mahogany in Boston, Newport, New York, Philadelphia, and Charleston. American Colonial is by far the most popular style of furniture reproduced today and original pieces are the most sought after.

American Empire. A ponderous, graceless style of furniture and decoration based on the French Empire styles of the Napoleonic era, which in turn were derived or adapted from Greek and Roman pieces, plus a strong Egyptian bias. Heavy pedestal tables, scroll sofas, sleigh beds, and massive bureaus and sideboards were further weighed down by excessive ornamentation and carving, sometimes gilded, that aped the French bronze appliqué. Even such leading cabinetmakers as Duncan Phyfe and Charles Honoré Lannuier abandoned the cool classicism of Directoire for this debased style. A typical American Empire room is shown on page 17.

American primitive paintings. The stylized, flat, linear paintings done by "limners," self-taught itinerant folk artists who traveled the countryside in the late eighteenth and nineteenth centuries, earning a living by painting family portraits, landscapes, scenes from daily life, history, and the Bible, and by decorating the walls of rooms. Some, like Winthrop Chandler and Ami Phillips, became successful enough to find sufficient commissions near home. Others did not even sign their work and have remained anonymous. At their best, these primitive paintings, one of which appears in the bedroom on page 42, exhibit a refreshing simplicity of vision and a vitality that has made them much admired and collected.

Antique. U.S. Customs regulations define as antique anything made one hundred or more years ago. However, the status of an "antique" is more often established by prevailing vogues—witness the recent upsurge of interest in Art Deco, a style of the 1920's and 1930's, with a corresponding rise in price.

Arrow back. A style of American Windsor chair with three or more arrow-shaped spindles in the back.

Art glass. All-inclusive term for various types of late nineteenth-century ornamental glass that were blown, blown-molded, or pressed into fancy forms and colors. Among the most collected (and expensive) are Amberina, Favrile, Peach Blow, and satin glass.

Art Moderne. French term for modern or contemporary design, used in the United States during the 1920's to describe the new breed of modern objects, now more commonly referred to as Art Deco (see page 29, center right).

Art Nouveau. Popularized by Henri van de Velde in Paris in 1895, this decorative style of art and architecture spread throughout Europe and America in the years until 1910, and had its own influence on its successor, Art Deco. Art Nouveau, which encouraged free but distorted interpretations of nature and was distinguished by sinuous, flowing lines, encompassed styles derived from the Gothic and the Japanese. Exemplars of the style are Van de Velde and Victor Horta in Europe, Louis Comfort Tiffany in America. Today, Art Nouveau pieces are widely copied and during the 1960's the style was successfully revived in decorative home furnishings. (For examples of Art Nouveau furnishings, see pages 98–99, page 138, bottom.)

Art Deco. A highly decorative style of art and architecture that held sway in America and Europe during the 1920's and 1930's (see page 29, top right), foreshadowed by Josef Hoffman's Palais Stoclet in Brussels and named for the 1925 Paris Exposition Internationale des Arts Décoratifs.

Art Deco was a jazzy mixture of widely disparate design influences, from Egyptian, Aztec, and American Indian to Regency, Art Nouveau, Bauhaus, and the hard, rectangular forms of Cubism. It was characterized by symmetrical, rectilinear forms and glossy surfaces in lacquered or polished wood, shiny metals, tiles, crystal, smoky glass, and such new materials as Bakelite and Vitrolite. Buildings in the Art Deco style were sheathed with glass, marble, bronze, and other metals, and lacquered wood. As an initial step in popularizing mass-produced modern, Art Deco merged art and industry in a successful marriage. Many well-known architects and decorators made their contributions, among them Frank Lloyd Wright, Eero Saarinen, and Jean-Michel Frank. The current rage for Art Deco started in the late 1960's, after the Louvre's Musée des Arts Décoratifs revived part of the 1925 show (see page 138, top).

Arts and Crafts Movement. In the late nineteenth century, the English artist and designer William Morris started this movement as a revolt against the stereotyped products of the machine age, forming a company to produce hand-crafted furnishings and accessories that would cover the whole field of design. In this country, his ideas and ideals were upheld by groups such as the Roycrofters in East Aurora, New York, the Craftsman Workshops near Syracuse, and the Rookwood Pottery in Cincinnati, Ohio.

Audubon, John James (1780–1851). Artist and ornithologist whose name is synonymous with prints of American birds. While the originals are rare and costly, reproductions of Audubon prints are common.

Authentic reproduction. A line-for-line copy of the original, such as the authorized Williamsburg reproduction furniture shown on pages 114 and 115.

B

Bachelor chest. A narrow chest of drawers for a man's clothing, with a fold-over top or pull-out shelf beneath the top for writing or toiletries. This type of chest, introduced during the Queen Anne period, had a great vogue in the eighteenth century and is currently reproduced.

Balloon back. Chair back attributed to Hepplewhite with a shape that swells out like a balloon. The design was adopted for rockers and side chairs in the nineteenth century (a balloon-back side chair is shown on page 25).

Ballroom chair. A small, lightweight gilt side chair, usually with bamboo turnings. Easy to transport, the chairs were rented en masse for balls and receptions, hence the name.

Bandbox. A round or oval box of pasteboard or thin strips of wood, painted or covered with paper, used in the nineteenth century to store hats. A collection of such bandboxes is shown on page 103.

Banjo clock. A popular banjo-shaped nineteenth-century wall clock invented and patented by Simon Willard of Roxbury, Massachusetts. It usually had a painted panel in the lower section, a stained or gilded wood frame, and a finial, shaped like an eagle or an urn, above the round dial, as seen in the living room on page 16, top.

Barn red. A popular American color, both out and indoors, ever since the early settlers painted their barns with a mixture of red iron oxide, linseed oil, and turpentine. Nowadays it is frequently found in "Early American" rooms, documentary fabrics, wallpapers, and mass-produced Colonial-style furniture.

Belter, John Henry. German-born cabinetmaker who worked in New York City from 1844 to the 1860's, producing some of the finest Victorian rococo furniture. Highly carved, mostly of rosewood, walnut, or oak, with brocade or damask upholstery, his pieces are distinguished by sinuous curves and heavy roll moldings. Belter is credited with developing and patenting a laminated wood process which made it possible to carve, bend, and shape panels of laminated rosewood veneer into the most intricate designs. Today, Belter furniture, examples of which can be seen on page 81, is highly prized for its superb craftsmanship.

Bennington. Familiar and widely collected mottled brown earthenware first made here in the nineteenth-century pottery of Norton and Fenton in Bennington, Vermont, hence the name, although it was originally made in England where it was known as Rockingham. American potteries throughout the country produced this ware, in everything from pie plates and teapots to door knobs, but it is mainly associated with the Vermont pottery, which also turned out pitchers and vases of Parian, an unglazed porcelain. (Parian figures are shown in a cabinet on page 104, top.)

Betty lamp. Early American iron or tin oil lamp, small, shallow, and pear-shaped, with a wick in the smaller end. It was hung from an iron rod on a stand or ratchet suspended from the ceiling.

Bible box. Originally, a plain or carved wood box that held the family Bible, with a slanting lid that served as a reading stand (see page 11, bottom). Later, it was mounted on legs and developed into a desk.

Bird-cage table. A tilt-top pedestal table with an openwork wood box, reminiscent of a bird cage, between top and base (see page 54, top).

Blanket chest. One of the most universal of all American storage pieces, the blanket chest was made in maple, cherry, and walnut, and often in painted or grained pine. It consisted of a lidded upper section and a drawer or drawers in the base (see page 11, top, and page 12, top).

Block front. A term applied to the front of a desk or chest which has three vertical panels, the center concave, the ends convex, as shown in the examples on pages 117 and 123. Panel tops end in carved shells. The design is attributed to John Goddard of Newport, Rhode Island.

Block printing. A form of printing practiced before the machine age and still current in the handcrafts field. A pattern or picture is hand-printed on paper or fabric with a series of carved wood blocks coated with dye, each of which produces one part of the design in a single flat color.

Blond finish. Chemical bleaching on medium-dark, open-grained woods such as mahogany produces this light tone. The wood is then treated with the usual furniture finishes. Blond finishes were extremely popular in the 1930's and early 1940's for the kind of furniture shown on pages 29 and 82.

Bonnet top. The arch contour, often broken, found on the top of such pieces of furniture as clocks, highboys, and secretaries (like the one on page 123), continuing from front to back.

Boston chair. A Restoration-style high-backed chair made in and around Boston in the eighteenth century. The frame was maple, often painted red or black, and the back and seat were either caned or covered with leather.

Boston rocker. A mid-nineteenth-century machine-made rocking chair with straight side posts and spindles, S-curved arms, and a wooden seat which curved up at the back and was rolled at the front, with slightly S-curved sides. This enduringly popular piece of Americana was usually painted and stenciled.

Bracket clock. A shelf or mantel clock with bracket feet, often with a matching wall bracket, popular in the eighteenth century.

Brewster chair. A rather elaborate turned-wood spindle chair named for Elder Brewster, one of the Pilgrim Fathers, and made from the 1600's until about 1725. The Brewster chair is characterized by double rows of spindles on the back, sides and at the front, under the seat. The Philadelphia Centennial of 1876 spurred a revival of this early colonial chair, and many copies can still be found.

Britannia ware. Mass-produced pewter, a popular look-alike for silver, from which the shapes were copied. Developed in England around 1750, it was extensively produced in America during the mid-nineteenth century.

Bull's-eye mirror. Circular ornamental mirror of the eighteenth and nineteenth centuries (see page 78). The glass was either convex or concave. When candle brackets are added, it is called a girandole. The most popular American types have eagle pediments and ball decoration around the glass.

Butterfly table. A popular Early American drop-leaf table with swinging brackets, resembling the wings of a butterfly, that support the leaves.

C

Campaign furniture. Originally designed for the military, and later adapted for the home, this versatile folding and portable furniture encompassed camp beds (folding cots), collapsible chairs for officers (now called director's chairs), folding stools with canvas slings, and the much-copied brass-handled campaign chest.

Candlestand. A small table with a tripod, pedestal, or four-legged base originally designed to hold a candlestick. Now, like the reproduction Shaker candlestand on page 113, it may be used as an occasional table.

Candlewick bedspread. Perennially popular type of spread made of heavy cotton yarn, or candlewick, where the relief design is either loom-woven or worked in by hand. Early candlewick spreads had loops and ridges. Later, these were clipped to give a tufted look. While most modern tufted candlewick spreads are machine-made, like the reproduction by Fieldcrest on page 47, some are still made by hand in the mountain states of the South.

Cannon-ball bed. A favorite of country cabinetmakers, this early nineteenth-century poster bed had four turned posts topped with a large ball (which gave the bed its name), a shaped headboard, and a blanket rail instead of a footboard.

Canton. See Chinese export porcelain.

Cape Cod lighter. An ingenious fire-lighting device consisting of a lidded metal container for kerosene (originally, whale oil) and a lighter of clay or other porous material attached to a metal handle. After the lighter had been soaked in the oil, it was ignited and put under the piled-up wood fire.

Captain's chair. A type of Windsor chair with high legs and a low, round spindle back in which nineteenth-century steamer captains were wont to sit while on the bridge or in the wheelhouse. Popular now in family rooms, or wherever sturdy, serviceable furniture is needed (see page 146, bottom).

Captain's decanter. Also called a ship decanter. A heavy cut- or blown-glass decanter with a wide, flat bell bottom designed to keep spirits from spilling when sailing ships rolled in heavy seas. Originally made in the eighteenth century, it is still a popular shape and is part of the Colonial Williamsburg line of reproductions.

Carnival glass. An inexpensive, iridescent glass, a poor man's copy of Favrile, so called because in the late nineteenth century it was given away at carnivals or for soap coupons. Also called taffeta glass.

Carver chair. A simpler version of the Brewster chair, with only one row of spindles across the back, turned posts, and a rush seat (for example, see page 49). It was named for John Carver, the first governor of the Massachusetts Bay Colony. Like the Brewster, this chair was also much copied in the late nineteenth century.

Cast-iron furniture. The first furniture specifically designed for use outdoors and indoors, mass-produced in the nineteenth century in a range of pieces from bedsteads, chairs, and garden benches to plant and umbrella stands and doorstops. While the originals are expensive, many are now being reproduced.

Cast-iron stove. Also mass-produced, the American nineteenth-century version of the cast-iron stove reflects the Victorian penchant for giving even the most utilitarian objects ornate surfaces and fanciful designs, ranging from the architectural to the neo-Gothic.

Cathedral clock. One of the more eccentric manifestations of the Victorian Gothic Revival, this type of clock had steeples, a peaked front, and was sometimes covered by a glass dome.

Chair table. Seventeenth-century form of dual-purpose furniture, a chair with a large circular or rectangular back that worked on pivots and could be pulled forward to rest on the arms, forming a table like the one on page 103. Also called a monk's chair. Versions in pine or maple are currently reproduced.

Chalkware. Inexpensive molded plaster of Paris figures, colored with water or oil paints and left unglazed. They were made in the latter part of the nineteenth century as a mass-market substitute for more costly pottery and porcelain figures. Although some chalkware was made in Boston as early as 1780, most of it was produced later, often by itinerant artisans who carried their materials with them. The Pennsylvania Dutch were especially expert at molding and painting these naive figures of domestic animals, such as cats, goats, and chickens, fruit and simple pastoral scenes. See examples on pages 103 and 183.

Cheval glass. A portable full-length mirror that swings from two posts fastened to a trestle. Smaller versions, designed to top a chest or table, have a drawer between the posts (see page 179, lower right).

Chinese export porcelain. Umbrella term covering a multitude of hard-paste porcelains made to order in China during the eighteenth and nineteenth centuries, specifically for the European and American markets, tables, and tastes. Some of the better-known patterns are Fitzhugh, Rose Medallion, and the familiar blue-and-white Canton or Nanking (so called because it was shipped through those ports), which, with its Chinese landscape of bridges, boats, and trees, was the inspiration for the English willow pattern. While Canton was regarded by wealthy Americans of the eighteenth century as everyday china, today it is a collector's item. (Canton that belonged to George Washington is shown in the butler's pantry at Mount Vernon on page 95.) At one point in the nineteenth century, export porcelain was dubbed Lowestoft, or Oriental Lowestoft, in the mistaken belief that it came from Lowestoft, England, a name that is still erroneously used.

Chippendale. The most outstanding of the Georgian styles, developed by the English master cabinet-maker and designer, Thomas Chippendale II (1740–1799). His influence can be seen in the furniture of the great eighteenth-century American cabinetmakers from Rhode Island to Charleston, as shown in chapter 6, and especially the school known as Philadelphia Chippendale.

Cigar-store Indian. Life-sized, carved, and brightly painted wooden Indians, used outside tobacco shops from the mid-nineteenth to early twentieth centuries as an eye-catching advertisement for their wares. Often the figure held wooden cigars extended on its palm, or clutched in its hand. Although there were other cigar-store figures— sailors, soldiers, Turks, Negroes—the Indians were most popular.

Cobbler's bench. Workmanlike piece of colonial furniture with a seat, bin, last holder, and tool compartment, now copied as a coffee table for Early American rooms.

Colonial. In America, the period from the earliest settlements to the Revolution, a designation sometimes mistakenly applied to furniture and accessories of American origin up to 1850.

Colonial Revival. In the late nineteenth century, a resurgence of interest in Colonial American architecture, furniture, and decoration brought about many adaptations and imitations of the early designs.

Comb back. A high back seen on Windsor chairs, with many spindles set like the teeth of a comb into a broad top rail (see page 183).

Connecticut chest. An Early American dower or storage chest made in the vicinity of the Connecticut River Valley. The chests, which were made of carved and painted oak and pine, had one or two drawers and a storage well below the lid. Typical examples are the sunflower-and-tulip chest, which has three panels carved with stylized flowers, and the Guildford chest, with an all-over polychrome design of leaves and flowers on the sides and front panel.

Constitution mirror. American mirror of the Sheraton type, dating from about 1791. It was usually gilded, with columns up the sides of the frame, a series of ball decorations under the cornice, and a painted panel below. In nineteenth-century versions, the panel often depicted the frigate *Constitution* in action during the War of 1812, hence the name (see page 51, upper right).

Convex wall mirror. This late eighteenth-century English circular mirror in the French Empire style had a carved and gilded frame embellished with classical motifs and surmounted by a spread eagle—which accounts for its adoption by and identification with the American Federal era, although actually most of the mirrors found in America came from England or France. (Two such mirrors are shown on pages 16 and 17.)

Copies. Replicas or reproductions of pieces from previous periods. In furniture, the scale may be altered to suit the size of modern rooms, or a detail may be omitted, but in general the copies are faithful to the originals.

Country Chippendale. A simple, transitional American country version of Chippendale, generally chairs (see page 51, lower left).

Country furniture. Unpretentious and charming furniture made by country craftsmen, much of it at home, in emulation of the more elegant pieces of the day, the American equivalent of European provincial styles. Local woods like pine and maple were used and often painted to simulate more expensive woods or decorative inlay, and design motifs were simplified. Most country furniture, like the examples on pages 24 and 25, was basically functional—cupboards and wardrobes, dower and blanket chests, beds, chairs, tables, desks, pie safes, and dry sinks. Some of the still-popular types of country chair are the slat-back, the Windsor, and the Hitchcock chair. The increasing demand for inexpensive furniture was responsible for factory-made spool furniture with its simple bulbous turnings on legs and frames. By 1860, Grand Rapids, Michigan, had taken over as the center of mass production, turning out simplified versions of more costly pieces in inexpensive oak. Much of the Grand Rapids painted "cottage furniture," like that on page 24, has continued in favor

and is now regarded as an authentic American antique.

Courting mirrors. Small mirrors with inlaid or painted glass frames brought to America from China by the crews of the clipper ships, as gifts for their sweethearts and wives. These mirrors are currently reproduced.

Cranberry glass. A simple nineteenth-century glassware distinguished by the color—a purple-tinged, pinky red produced by the addition of gold oxide to the molten glass.

Currier and Ives. Nathaniel Currier, who set up business in New York in 1834, and James Merritt Ives, who became his partner in 1857, have rightly been called "printmakers to the American people." Their colored lithographs, drawn by a number of different artists, constitute a graphic record of the events and scenes of life in nineteenth-century America, and have been widely reproduced. The prints, which vary from postcard size to large folio, were hand-colored until 1880, after which time they were mostly printed in colors from a series of stones.

D

Daguerreotypes. The earliest photographs, an invention of the Frenchman, Louis Daguerre, in 1839. There are three types: daguerreotypes on silver, ambrotypes on glass, and tintypes on collodion-coated iron.

Davenport. Common U.S. term for an upholstered sofa. The Davenport table, or sofa table, was placed behind the davenport, away from the wall.

Deacon's bench. American name for a Windsor settee with four back divisions contoured like chair backs.

Dish-top table. Similar to the piecrust table, but with a bead-molded rim like that on a pewter dish, about half an inch high. A popular piece of American furniture, made chiefly in maple, cherry, walnut, and mahogany.

Distelfink. Popular bird-form found in the folk art and painted decoration of the Pennsylvania Dutch, loosely patterned on the goldfinch. In direct translation, thistle finch.

Documentary. A reproduction of a design taken from an antique or old fabric or wallpaper, either a faithful copy of the original or a rescaled or recolored version.

Dower chest. Two distinct types of this bride's hope chest were produced in America. One was the carved and painted Connecticut chest, the other the chest of the Pennsylvania Dutch (shown on page 12, top), decorated according to the county of origin with geometric or stylized motifs, figures, riders, animals, and sometimes the name of the owner.

Dresser. In America, a chest of drawers, usually with a mirror attached, used in a bedroom. The English dresser is a type of sideboard with open shelves and cupboards.

Dry sink. A nineteenth-century cupboard with a recessed well lined in metal. As the dry sink had no plumbing, water was brought to it when dishes had to be washed. Today, the dry sink may hold plants or act as a bar.

Dutch Colonial. Architecture and furnishings associated with the seventeenth-century Dutch who settled on Long Island and in the Hudson River valley. The style, based on simplified baroque, is heavy but pleasing. One of the more noteworthy pieces was the kas, or chest, shown on page 11; this was often decoratively painted.

E

Eagle motif. Since the days of the Romans, countries glorying in their martial successes have taken the eagle either whole or in part—head, wings and feet—as a decorative symbol. During the American Federal period, the feet supported couches, and the carved and gilded bird topped mirrors. Today, the eagle motif mostly appears on copies of antiques or as a decorative overdoor or plaque.

Eastlake. Gothic and Jacobean Revival furniture designed by the English architect and designer, Charles Locke Eastlake, whose *Hints on Household Taste*, published in 1867, was immensely popular and influential in America. The furniture, mostly of oak or cherry, was machine-made and embellished with shallow carving, dark trimming, panels of tile or inlay, heavy hardware, and metal mounts.

Eclecticism. When properly handled, one of the more interesting and successful ways to decorate a room, using an uninhibited mixture of styles in furniture and accessories drawn from different periods and countries. (For examples of the Eclectic Look, see pages 34 and 75.)

Elfe, Thomas (1719–1775). Leading cabinetmaker of Charleston, South Carolina, active from 1747 to 1775, during which time his establishment turned out great quantities of furniture in the Queen Anne and Chippendale styles. His work was characterized by a band of applied fret in a hori-

zontal looped design on desks, chests of drawers, and bookcases. Reproductions of Elfe's work are shown on pages 119 and 123.

F

Fan-back chair. Chair with spindles that radiate in a fan shape, as in the fan-backed Windsor chair.

Fancy chairs. Early nineteenth-century American take-offs of European designs, such as the Sheraton-inspired Hitchcock chair, shown on page 123.

Favrile glass. Iridescent late nineteenth-century case glass noted for exotic colors and fanciful shapes. Best known is the Favrile of Louis Comfort Tiffany, more generally known as Tiffany glass (see pages 98–99), but other types were made in this country, such as Durand and Aurene.

Federal (1780–1830). This patriotic style of the transitional era from the Revolution to Victorian-age America embraced a welter of design influences, both imported and native, starting with the neo-Classic. The early Federal furniture made from about 1790 to 1815, known as American Sheraton, is light and refined, with strong evidences of Sheraton, Adam, and French Directoire. Samuel McIntire excelled in interpretations of Adam, while the best work of Duncan Phyfe was in the manner of French Directoire and late Sheraton. Late Federal (from 1815 to 1840) furniture came under the more grandiose influence of French Empire and coincided with the Greek Revival in architecture. Most Federal furniture was made of mahogany, with curly maple used to imitate the English satinwood. After the War of 1812, the eagle became the dominant and patriotic motif on furniture, mirrors, clocks, even china and glass.

During the Federal period, there was great interest in archaeology and classic architecture, reflected in the pure lines and beautiful detail of the interiors of Thomas Jefferson's home, Monticello (see pages 67, 68 and 69). The best examples of Federal furniture are currently being reproduced by such firms as Kittinger (see pages 120 and 121).

Fiddleback. Chair in the Queen Anne style that took its name from the shape of the back splat, reminiscent of a violin (see page 43, lower right). Popular since the colonial days.

Figurehead. Carved and brightly painted wood figures that adorned the bows of American sailing ships. On the clipper ships, these were mostly of bosomy women, sometimes models of a member of the captain's family, while military vessels had figureheads of eagles or national heroes (President Andrew Jackson was the choice for the frigate *Constitution*). Figureheads, either old or reproduction, are now often seen mounted on the walls of family rooms.

Fireboard. A decorative device employed in the old days to close off the unused fireplace in summer. The made-to-measure wood panel, often canvas-covered, was painted with a scene or floral still-life, sometimes with a painted trompe-l'oeil frame.

Four-poster. American term for a bed with four elongated corner posts, but no wood canopy.

Fractur. The hand-illuminated script with which the Pennsylvania Dutch adorned their birth, baptism, marriage, and death certificates. Written in German, the certificates were highly decorated with motifs like angels, hearts, flowers, birds, and gold initials. Now regarded as an authentic, engaging form of folk art, they are much prized by collectors (see page 12, top).

Franklin stove. One of Benjamin Franklin's more enduring inventions, this cast-iron wood-burning stove-cum-fireplace (also known as the Pennsylvania fireplace) is still around in several of its many versions, as a working or decorative addition to rooms.

Fretwork mirror. Chippendale-style American wall mirror of late eighteenth-century vintage. The wood frame had a fret-scrolled, arched crest, often with a central motif, such as a shell, and a fret-cut base. It was also called a silhouette mirror.

Frothingham, Benjamin (1734–1809). American cabinetmaker who established a business in Charlestown, Massachusetts, in 1756. He is best known for his mahogany block-front furniture (see page 123), which had a more rounded quality and simpler ornamentation than that of the Goddard–Townsend group.

G

Gaudy Dutch. Also known as Gaudyware or Gaudy Welsh. An inexpensive Staffordshire earthenware imitation of the colorful floral Imari designs, produced in the nineteenth century by Derby, Worcester, and other English factories. As this ware was much favored and used in the Pennsylvania Dutch country, it was mistakenly assumed that it came from there, hence the name. The designs were executed in bright red, blue, and yellow applied over the glaze, with some parts either painted under the glaze or transfer-printed.

The Pfalzgraff Company of York, Pennsylvania, is currently reproducing a line of Gaudy Dutch tableware from the collection of the Henry Ford Museum in Dearborn, Michigan.

Gentleman's chair. An upholstered balloon-back armchair, part of the Victorian living-room set, which was completed by a matching, but smaller and armless, lady's chair, a medallion-back sofa and six side chairs (for examples, see pages 18 and 64).

Goddard and Townsend. Some of the finest of the late eighteenth-century American furniture came from the Goddards and the Townsends, a two-family group of Newport cabinetmakers headed by John Goddard and his son-in-law, John Townsend. Among the more distinctive Goddard and Townsend pieces, many of which are still reproduced, are the block-front chests, desks, and secretaries with shell carving (see page 117).

Gostelowe, Jonathan (1744–1795). A Philadelphia cabinetmaker with a wealthy clientele who specialized in the finest quality mahogany furniture with a strong strain of Chippendale Baroque.

Governor Winthrop desk. An American eighteenth-century fall-front desk in the Chippendale style, with graduated drawers on bracket feet and, in the writing section, small drawers and pigeonholes. Despite the name, it is highly unlikely that any of the several Governors Winthrop ever owned this desk, since they were around a good century before it appeared.

Grand Rapids style. A term that has become synonymous with the mass-produced "golden oak" furniture turned out by factories in Grand Rapids, Michigan, and other parts of the country at the turn of the century. Lately, this has been taken up as a kind of camp antique furniture (see page 146, top).

Greek Revival. A Federal style of architecture and furniture spawned by the great wave of interest in Greek classicism that swept through western Europe in the late eighteenth and early nineteenth centuries. Architectural columns and moldings, furniture, statues, urns, and various art forms were copied for the homes of the wealthy. The furniture of Duncan Phyfe shows evidences of this neo-classic influence (see page 15, lower left).

H

Hadley chest. An early New England oak chest with a hinged top, short legs, and from one to three drawers, crudely carved in simple floral motifs, often with the owner's initials on the center panel. It is credited to Captain John Allis of Hadley, Massachusetts.

Handkerchief table. American drop-leaf table which takes its name from the triangular top resembling a handkerchief folded corner to corner. When the drop-leaf is raised, the table turns square.

Harvest table. An American country dining table, long and narrow, with one or two shallow drop leaves, at which farmhands were seated at harvest time.

Hepplewhite. Named for designer and cabinetmaker George Hepplewhite, this graceful eighteenth-century English furniture was inspired chiefly by classic sources and the prevailing Louis XV styles. Shield backs, fluted legs and spade feet, curves, and a sparing use of carving, generally classical, are characteristic of the Hepplewhite style, which had a certain influence on American craftsmen of the Federal period, although that of Sheraton was stronger.

Hikie. A low, wide, armless, and backless type of contemporary lounging and sleeping piece which originated in Hawaii (see page 136, lower right). It may well have come from the crude Polynesian bed—piled-up layers of lauhala mattresses.

Hitchcock chair. The widely copied chair mass-produced by the early nineteenth-century cabinetmaker, Lambert Hitchcock. Based on a Sheraton original, the chair has a broad pillow-back band, turned and splayed legs, and a rush or cane seat, and is usually painted and frequently stenciled with fruit, flowers, or patriotic motifs. See example on page 123.

Hoop back. Chair back with a rail that forms a continuous hooplike curve, common in Windsor chairs.

Horn furniture. Fantasy furniture made of horns and antlers, originally intended for nineteenth-century hunting lodges and trophy rooms. There are four basic types of horn furniture, mostly importations, although some was made in the Far West from the 1860's. Taken up again in the late 1960's by interior designers and those with a taste for Victoriana, the furniture is longer on looks than comfort. For an example, see page 98.

Hunt board. An American sideboard of the early nineteenth century of a height appropriate for self-service at hunt breakfasts.

Hunt table. The forerunner of the hunt board (which was additionally equipped with drawers), this long or crescent-shaped sideboard table had drop leaves to extend the serving surface. The main feature is the height, designed to be stood, rather than sat, around. Today, the hunt table is used as a serving buffet, a desk (as shown on page 61), or, lowered, as a coffee table.

Hutch. A chest or cabinet topped by an open shelf deck, a popular sideboard in early colonial households.

I

Ironstone. A thick, heavy white china that originally contained slag from iron mines. Patented in England by James Mason of Staffordshire in 1814, it has been popular in America since it was first made here in the 1860's. While the plain white dinner services are the most familiar, some early ironstone was hand-painted with floral designs or decorated with colored transfer printing.

J

Japanning. A Western imitation of oriental lacquer in which layers of colored varnish were applied to the surface of wood, metal, or other materials, such as papier mâché, to give a hard, lustrous finish. Much of the old painted American domestic tinware, or tole, was japanned, and then baked to fix the finish (see page 95, bottom, page 97, right). This technique reached its height of popularity in the beginning of the nineteenth century, especially in Pennsylvania and the Northeast.

Jenny Lind bed. A small spool bed with low head and foot boards, dubbed Jenny Lind for the famous soprano, who happened to be touring the United States for P. T. Barnum at the time it was in vogue.

Jigsaw mirror. A mirror with a scrolled frame, originally cut by hand, later with a jigsaw, popular in eighteenth- and nineteenth-century America.

K

Kas. The large wood cupboard of the early Dutch settlers. It was usually made of pine, oak, walnut, cherry, or maple, and ornamented with carving, paneling, and painted decoration (see page 11, bottom).

Kettle base. American name for a chest curved like a kettle, swelling outward at the sides, front, or both, a shape more generally described by the French word, bombé (see page 53, top right).

L

Lady's chair. Victorian companion to the gentleman's chair, also upholstered and balloon-backed, but armless, to accommodate the hooped skirts of the day.

Lannuier, Charles Honoré. French cabinetmaker who worked in New York from 1805 to 1819 in the

Directoire and early Empire styles. Many of his pieces are in the main rooms of the White House. A Lannuier bed is shown on page 15.

Lighthouse clock. Nineteenth-century American shelf clock, with a shape vaguely resembling a lighthouse. The brass dial and works are covered by a glass dome set on a tapering body and octagonal plinth with a small door.

Lincoln rocker. An upholstered rocking chair with a high back, open arms, and gracefully curved wood frame, so named because Abraham Lincoln owned one.

Lowboy. A low chest or table with drawers, originating in Jacobean England and popular in eighteenth-century America, where it was used as a dressing table or writing table.

Lyre motif. A decorative shape of the ancient Greeks that reoccurred during classical revivals. It is found in Duncan Phyfe chair backs and table bases and furniture of the American Empire period (see page 15, lower right).

M

Mallard, Prudent. Born in Sèvres and trained in France, Mallard arrived in New York City in 1829, where he is believed to have worked with Duncan Phyfe. Moving to New Orleans, he opened a shop on Royal Street in 1838 and became one of the most fashionable cabinetmakers, especially noted for his rosewood and marble bedroom furniture and carved half-testers. His designs, strongly influenced by Renaissance and Louis XV rococo, were embellished with carving, moldings, and applied ornaments, frequently of lemonwood on rosewood. Mallard's furniture was well suited to the lavish ante-bellum homes and plantations of the South.

Martha Washington chair. An open-arm chair with a high, straight upholstered back, upholstered seat, and wooden arms, like the reproduction shown on page 114.

McIntire, Samuel (1757–1811). American architect and wood carver of Salem, Massachusetts. While McIntire was chiefly famous for his mantelpieces and overdoors, many of which are currently reproduced, he also contributed to the Federal design period beautifully carved, delicate furniture in the Adams style, like the bed shown on page 80.

Martha Washington table. An oval sewing or work table with two or three center drawers fitted for sewing necessities, and ends with hinged tops over rounded bins for storing work in progress. It was made in the Hepplewhite, Sheraton, and American Empire styles in the late eighteenth and early nineteenth centuries.

Mercury glass. Silvered glass made during the mid-nineteenth century to ape silver. The interior of the double-blown glass was coated with silver nitrate and the exterior sometimes etched or decorated. Mercury glass, both new and old, had a spurt of popularity in the 1970's, when the vogue for metallic and silvery surfaces was at its height.

Mission. American machine-made furniture popular at the turn of the century, similar in appearance to the pioneer furniture fashioned of native materials by the Spanish friars and Indians of the Southwest and California. The furniture was heavy, usually made of dark-stained oak, with nail-studded leather upholstery on the chairs. The originator of the style, Gustav Stickley, a furniture manufacturer who became a disciple of William Morris, called the furniture Craftsman, but it is more generally known as Mission.

Mocha ware. Mocha-colored earthenware with contrasting bands of daubed decoration, originally made in England in the mid-1800's and widely copied in America.

Moderne. A popular furniture style of the 1920's, loosely based on simplified Hepplewhite designs and characterized by blond finishes, straight lines, tubular metal frames, and wood grains and inlays for contrast.

Modernistic. Term for the exaggerated, jazzy architecture and decoration of the late 1920's and early 1930's, an offshoot of Art Deco. Shapes were stepped, zigzagged, and angular, furniture overblown and over-upholstered; bleached woods were combined with glass, shiny metals, and the newly discovered plastics (see page 29, center, page 82, top, page 139, top). This Hollywood-set look, often carried out in shades of white or pastels, is with us again today, in a more sophisticated rendering.

Mourning pictures. One of the more bizarre forms of nineteenth-century American folk art, these embroidered *memento mori* were usually lachrymose depictions of an urn or monument inscribed to the deceased, surrounded by grieving relatives beneath a weeping willow. Later, ink and watercolors were combined with embroidery, and finally the needlework was replaced by painting and stenciling.

Mule chest. An early American form of storage with one or more drawers beneath the lid and sometimes side handles for transportation.

N

Navajo rugs. Rugs made by the Navajo Indians, who were taught weaving by the Spanish priests. The first rugs were in a plain weave and natural-color wools, patterned with grey, white, and black stripes. Later, when the Indians learned to extract a red dye from tree bark and to barter for indigo, color was introduced. By the nineteenth century, the symbolic motifs, chevrons, and diamonds, were combined with straight border design. While today's Navajo rugs are still made in these traditional patterns, the yarns, dyes, and color combinations reflect the influence of commercialism.

Newport School. A group of eighteenth-century Rhode Island cabinetmakers of whom the best known are John Goddard, Job Townsend, and Townsend's sons, John and Job Edward. (See Goddard and Townsend.)

P

Painted furniture. Simple country furniture, painted to protect, decorate, or disguise the surface of inexpensive native woods like pine, oak, and maple, has been part of American interiors since the days of the first settlers. Typical examples are the Dutch kas, with its realistic designs of fruit, flowers, and birds; the Pennsylvania Dutch schrank, or wardrobe, and dower chest; the blanket chests of New England and some of the early Windsor chairs, designed for outdoor use and painted green or black. Decoration ranged from natural forms and stylized motifs to simulated graining and patterns made with sponges and feathers. Later, when stenciling was adopted as a quick, cheap substitute for hand-painting and gilding, the mass-produced Hitchcock chair made its appearance, to be followed at the turn of the century by the Grand Rapids painted cottage furniture with decorations of nosegays and wreaths (the kind shown on page 24, bottom).

Papier-mâché. Molded, glued, and lacquered paper, a material much used in nineteenth-century America for tables, side chairs, trays, and boxes. Papier-mâché was usually black, with inlaid mother-of-pearl decorations in oriental designs.

Parlor lamp. A late nineteenth-century oil lamp with a globular base and shade of china or glass, often brilliantly colored, with painted, etched or decal decoration, and a brass base. Known to us as the "Gone with the Wind" lamp because of its use in the movie sets (see page 30), although actually it was not around in Civil War days.

Parsons table. A square or rectangular table with apron and leg widths of the same measurement. It originated at, and was named for, the Parsons School of Design. Versions of the table, which is akin in design to early Chinese tables, were conceived independently in New York and Paris by Joseph Platt and Jean-Michel Frank. The overwhelmingly popular Parsons table comes in a wide range of sizes. It can be found in the lines of many furniture manufacturers and, unpainted, in stores that sell simple, inexpensive, unfinished furniture.

Patchwork. Although the piecing together of scraps of different fabrics originated with the Egyptians and flourished in the Middle Ages, when walls and beds had coverings and hangings of velvet patchwork, this thrifty domestic art is particularly identified with America, beginning with the patchwork quilts of the New England settlers. Patchwork became a decorative art in the eighteenth and nineteenth centuries and today it has seen a revival in both actual patchwork and brightly colored patchwork designs printed on wallpaper and fabric. For today's patchwork look, see page 129.

Peacock chair. A style of rattan chair from Hong Kong with a high, lacy, fan back and hourglass-shaped base that has been popular since Victorian days (see page 26). Often called the "Saratoga" chair, after the spa in New York State where it was standard seating for hotel porches.

Pencil-post bed. A popular Queen Anne poster bed with slim, octagonal posts that tapered toward the top. While the foot posts were mostly carved or reeded, the head posts were left plain, as the bed curtains covered them (see page 25).

Pennsylvania Dutch. The early German and Swiss settlers in eastern Pennsylvania (Dutch is a local corruption of Deutsch), who were noted for a style of naive painted decoration in clear, strong colors, mostly fanciful motifs of fruit and flowers, animals, birds, and people, with which they embellished their furniture, utensils, and rooms. In addition to forthright, sturdy domestic furniture, some of the more interesting, characteristic, and decorative pieces are the bridal or dower chests, hanging cabinets, dough troughs, boxes of all kinds, a wide range of painted tinware, and the highly individual fractur paintings. (For an example of Pennsylvania Dutch decoration, see the room on page 12.)

Period color scheme. A color scheme taken from that of a historical period and applied to a contemporary room. Aided by painstaking and authentic restorations such as Williamsburg, American manufacturers have been able to reproduce exactly the colors and patterns of paint, wallpaper, and fabric which, combined with furniture reproductions like those shown in chapter 6, make it an easy matter to reconstruct or reinterpret a period room.

Duncan Phyfe (1768–1854). America's first great furniture designer, whose style was derived in part from English and French design of the period. His earliest work, done in Albany, New York, was in the manner of Adam and Hepplewhite. After moving his workshop to New York City around 1790, he developed a trade in custom designs based on Sheraton and French Directoire, which we know as Federal (see examples on pages 15 and 80). Phyfe's most characteristic motif is the classical lyre, which is found in his chair backs and table bases. Most of his furniture was mahogany, although later pieces were made of rosewood.

Piecrust table. Descriptive name for a round, tilt-top pedestal table with a carved or molded scalloped edge. Of English origin, the piecrust table was made by American cabinetmakers from around 1750 to 1770, in Connecticut of cherry, and in Philadelphia of mahogany.

Pier glass. A type of tall wall mirror that was hung in the space (or pier) between windows, usually over a low, marble-topped console or pier table (see pages 18–19).

Pillar and scroll clock. A type of mantel clock introduced by Eli Terry of Plymouth, Connecticut, widely copied by other clockmakers and reproduced today. It resembles the upper part of a tall case clock, with a scrolled top and base, side columns, and a scene painted on glass below the square enameled dial (see page 114).

Pineapple motif. This symbol of hospitality can be seen in the eighteenth-century houses of Newport, Rhode Island, as a finial in the broken pediment over the front door, and atop bed posts. Today, the motif is printed on fabrics and wallpapers, or appears in lamp and table bases.

Platform rocker. An upholstered chair of the Eastlake persuasion invented around 1870. The seat is attached to a platform by yoke springs, on which it rocks.

Pressed glass. Mass-produced glass introduced around 1825 by American manufacturers, so called because instead of being blown, the glass was shaped by pressure in a mold. Because of this inexpensive process, sets of glass tableware could be sold for a moderate cost. The earliest type was called lace or lacy glass, for the background stippling of raised dots that gave a fine, lace-like effect. The later, unstippled type was called pattern glass. Many hundreds of different patterns were turned out by factories in New England, New York, New Jersey and Pennsylvania, the best known being the Sandwich factory (see page 96, top). Today, pressed glass is being reproduced from old molds.

Puritan furniture. A simple functional style of the New England Puritan colonists, based on English Cromwellian pieces (see page 12, bottom).

Q

Queen Anne style. The furniture that developed during the reign of Queen Anne in England (1702–1714), easily recognized by its undulating lines, cabriole legs, and chair backs with a single curved splat, fiddle- or vase-shaped and spooned to fit the back. It was the first designed for domestic comfort and such relaxing amenities as the taking of afternoon tea. Queen Anne was immensely popular in America, where adaptations of the style were made from 1720 to 1750 in such centers of fine craftsmanship as Philadelphia, Boston, Newport, New York, and Charleston. Typical American pieces are the highboy with cabriole legs and scrolled pediment, and the Windsor chair.

Quilts. The bedcover elevated to a domestic art, American pieced and appliqué quilts have been made since the earliest colonial days, although most of the surviving examples of old quilts are from the nineteenth century. The pieced type consists of scraps of fabric (usually worn-out clothes) sewn together and then quilted to a backing, with a thin insulating layer of cotton or wool in between, like the familiar patchwork quilt, or the crazy quilt, which had no set design.

For the appliqué quilt, the fabric scraps were sewn directly onto a cloth backing in patterns ranging from simple, repetitive stylized designs (see page 129, bottom) to elaborate pictures and panels, occasionally combined with embroidery. Many quilts featured regional or symbolic motifs, such as Pennsylvania's tulip design, the Princess Feather, Rose of Sharon, and Star of Bethlehem. Album or friendship quilts, consisting of a series of blocks, each by a different woman in a different design, were usually made as engagement or bridal gifts.

R

Rag rugs. Hooked, braided, and woven rag rugs were one way for the careful nineteenth-century housewife to recycle old clothing. (While they are today associated with "Early American" rooms, it is unlikely that they were made in colonial times, when floors were usually left bare.)

For hooked rugs, long strips of cloth or yarn are drawn through a coarse backing such as burlap or canvas with a metal hook. For braided rugs, the strips are plaited, coiled, and sewn onto the backing. For woven rugs, the rags are hand-loomed with heavy cotton or linen as a warp.

Randolph, Benjamin. American cabinetmaker who worked in Philadelphia between 1750 and 1780, producing chairs and highboys in the Chippendale style.

Rayo lamp. The simplest of mass-produced kerosene lamps, with a nickel or brass-plated font and stand and a green glass shade. Survivals are electrified for use today.

Regency. An English style of the late Georgian era, when George IV was Prince Regent and King, strongly influenced by French Directoire and Empire, with certain distinctive Egyptian and Chinese motifs, notably bamboo trimming and caned seats and backs. Many pieces of the Federal period reflect the Regency style and much of today's bamboo-turned furniture is adapted from Regency designs.

Reproductions. Faithful copies of old pieces that duplicate all details and even the finish and patina, as shown in chapter 6. The word "reproduction" is today often applied more loosely to commercial pieces that have some of the feeling of the original, even though materials and proportions have been changed.

Restoration. The term for furniture, houses, or rooms that have been restored to their original condition, with any missing or damaged parts replaced, or substitutions made. While restored rooms and houses can re-create the past quite permissibly, restored furniture has much less value.

Rocking chair. This American invention attributed to Benjamin Franklin has been our favorite form of soothing seating since the eighteenth century. Typical examples are the Boston and Salem rockers, derived from the Windsor chair; the Victorian upholstered Lincoln rocker; the bentwood rocker; platform rockers; and the metal-framed upholstered rockers known as "digestive chairs."

Rogers groups. These mass-produced plaster groups of Civil War themes, historical figures, and scenes of everyday life designed by John Rogers from about 1860 were one of the most popular items of Victorian decor. Later derided, they are now prized by collectors.

Rookwood pottery. One-of-a-kind, hand-thrown pottery, characterized by rich, glowing underglaze colors and flowing forms, from the Rookwood factory in Ohio, a late nineteenth-century outgrowth of the Arts and Crafts Movement.

S

Salem secretary. American name for a type of Sheraton-style secretary–bookcase. The Salem secretary had a recessed upper section of bookshelves behind glazed doors, a projecting lower section with two or three rows of drawers, and occasionally a fall-front writing flap. The lower part of the recessed section sometimes concealed small drawers and pigeonholes.

Samplers. The early eighteenth-century samplers, which consisted of rows of different stitches, were basically samples of a little girl's progress in needlework, a necessary and lauded accomplishment. Gradually, they became elaborate pictures of houses, birds, animals, people, and flowers, usually framed in a border, with a little verse or uplifting maxim and the maker's age and name at the bottom.

Sandwich glass. Pressed glass originally made in Sandwich, Massachusetts, between 1825 and 1888, although the name is often mistakenly applied to pressed glass made by other factories. Reproductions of Sandwich glass are being made from the old molds.

Savery, William (1721–1787). A Philadelphia cabinetmaker who produced America's most elaborate and highly ornamented Chippendale-style furniture, from highboys and lowboys to mahogany and maple chairs and serpentine chests of drawers.

Sawbuck table. A large wooden table with two X-shaped supports. Although usually associated with early American interiors, this was originally a Gothic design. Contemporary versions of this table have steel or chrome supports, glass or marble tops. See trestle table.

Schoolmaster's desk. An early nineteenth-century teacher's desk, usually of painted pine, with a slant-top lid over a deep well, with a drawer underneath, both of which locked.

Schrank. The Pennsylvania Dutch name for the large cupboard the Dutch called a kas.

Scrimshaw. The art of engraving scenes on whalebone and whale teeth, or fashioning them into piecrust cutters or jewelry that was pursued by New England sailors of the eighteenth and nineteenth centuries to pass time on long whaling voyages and create gifts for their families or sweethearts. The incised designs were filled with rubbings of colored inks or lampblack. With whales now considered an endangered species, scrimshaw may soon become a lost art.

Settee. Long seat or bench with open arms and back. It may be upholstered, like the Sheraton settee, caned, like the Duncan Phyfe version, or painted and stenciled, as in the Hitchcock settee.

Settle. All-wood settee with solid arms and back, usually with a boxlike base below a hinged seat.

Shaker. Named for the Shakers, followers of an English religious sect who fled to America in the late eighteenth century, this simple, straightforward furniture made between 1776 and 1880, mainly of pine, walnut, maple, or fruitwoods, has a clean-lined, no-nonsense functionalism that has never dated (see examples on pages 23 and 60). The Shaker influence is apparent in much of today's furniture design. Reproductions of Shaker pieces, shown on page 113, are as popular today as ever.

Shaw, John. American cabinetmaker who worked in Annapolis, Maryland, from 1773 to 1794. His furniture was strongly influenced by the designs of Sheraton and Hepplewhite—chairs with modified shield backs, serpentine sideboards, and the typically English block feet (see page 123).

Sleepy Hollow chair. Nineteenth-century American upholstered chair that supposedly took its name from Washington Irving's home on the Hudson. Contoured for comfort, it had a deep, curved back, hollowed seat, low arms, and a companion ottoman or footstool.

Sleigh bed. The American version of the French Empire bed, with high, scrolled ends resembling a sleigh front.

Southern hunt board. A simply designed tall sideboard with long tapering legs, typical of country furniture made from local woods in the Southern states during the eighteenth and nineteenth centuries. The front is straight, with either a center cupboard flanked by drawers, or drawers flanked by cupboards.

South Jersey glass. Eighteenth-century American blown glass made in the German tradition at the southern New Jersey factory founded by Caspar Wistar in 1739. Later, glass of this type was also made in New England, New York, Pennsylvania, and Ohio.

Spice chest. A chest of many miniature drawers, developed in America in the eighteenth century to keep costly spices under lock and key. The chests vary considerably in style, length, and height.

Sponge painting. An early nineteenth-century form of fantasy finish in which the plain surface of wood furniture was decorated with paint applied with a sponge.

Steamboat Gothic. The jigsaw-cut wood "gingerbread"—balls, finials, gables, turnings, etc.—that adorned the inside and outside of Victorian houses and buildings (like the one on pages 176–177) derived this name from the elaborate trimmings of the Mississippi and Hudson River steamboats. Today, gingerbread salvaged from the wreckers is incorporated into screens, panels, and room dividers.

Stenciling. Surface decoration applied by brushing paint, stain, or dye through the cut-out openings of a paper pattern. Our ancestors used this easy and inexpensive way to add color and pattern to their plain rooms—on floors, walls, furniture, around windows and doors, on picture and mirror frames, boxes, and floorcloths, the painted canvas coverings that were used in place of woven rugs or as summer substitutes for heavier carpeting. Today, the technique of stenciling is being revived in contemporary colors and designs, with kits for those who don't wish to cut their own stencils. (For old and new examples of stenciling, see pages 42 and 56.)

Stiegel glass. Table and ornamental glassware originally made at the Manheim, Pennsylvania, factory of German-born Henry William Stiegel, the best known of all American eighteenth-century glassmakers. The glass was both free-blown and blown-molded, clear and colored (blue, yellow, red, and green), engraved and enameled. Authentic Stiegel glass is rare and expensive, but it has been widely copied and reproduced.

Student lamp. Late nineteenth-century oil lamp with a brass stem and base and a shade of tole or glass (usually green with a white lining) balanced by a fuel tank. Electrified versions of this popular lamp are made today. A rare example of a hanging student lamp is shown on page 100, by the sofa.

Stumpwork. Pictures embroidered in silk, with the design padded and stitched to stand out in relief, like trapunto, or quilting. A domestic art of Restoration England, revived in nineteenth-century America.

Sugar chest. A type of chest made for Southern plantation houses which had a very specific purpose—the safekeeping of sugar and similar luxury foods like tea, coffee, and spices. The chest was fitted with bins set in a lockable deep well below an overhanging top; it also had a drawer that locked.

T

Tester. The wood canopy of a four-poster bed, which may be carved or painted and either exposed or covered in fabric to match the hangings.

Theorems. A nineteenth-century form of stencil painting, considered a proper artistic form for young ladies. The paintings, frequently still-lifes of fruit and flowers, were done in watercolor, or in oils on velvet, with the stencils combined to form an individual design.

Tiffany glass. See Favrile. Examples are shown on pages 98–99 and 105.

Tole. Shaped and painted tin or other metalware, used for lamps, chandeliers, trays, occasional tables, boxes. Collections of tole are shown on pages 95 and 97.

Transfer. An eighteenth-century substitute for hand painting in which a picture printed in reverse on paper is transferred to an object such as a piece of china or furniture by first sticking the paper on and then peeling it off, leaving the picture behind. Staffordshire ware is decorated with transfer scenes. Today it is mainly found on children's furniture. Also known as decalcomania.

Treenware. Wooden objects, both utilitarian and decorative, turned by cabinetmakers and carpenters. Much of this ware was intended for kitchen use—spoons, ladles, rolling pins, tumblers, and cups—but there were also treen toys, caskets, boxes, bowls, urns, and epergnes.

Trencher. A large platter or flat serving plate of wood or metal, used by the American colonists, which derives its name from the French *tranche*, or slice, the thick hunk of bread that stood in for a plate in the Middle Ages.

Trestle table. Also known as a sawbuck table, this was originally a primitive Gothic dining table consisting of a heavy board or planks laid across trestles, so the table could be easily dismantled after use, or moved around.

Trundle bed. A low bed on casters designed in the Middle Ages to roll under a full-sized bed when not in use. This space-saving sleeping arrangement was widely used in colonial America, especially for children.

Tucker. American soft-paste porcelain imitation of Sèvres made in the Philadelphia factory of William Ellis Tucker between 1826 and 1838, now rare and prized by collectors. The china was decorated with flowers and gilding, monograms, coats of arms, and portraits of famous Americans, such as Washington.

Tufft, Thomas. Eighteenth-century Philadelphia cabinetmaker noted for his simple but well-styled lowboys.

U

Upstyled. An old design updated by being reinterpreted in contemporary terms (an example is the bed on page 57, bottom).

V

Victorian. Nineteenth-century medley of furniture styles and revivals that coincided with, and is named for, the lengthy reign of Queen Victoria, from the 1830's to the beginning of the twentieth century. Much Victorian furniture, developed from English and American Empire designs, was clumsy, heavily scaled and over ornamented. The best was the rococo furniture of John Belter. Revivals ran the gamut from Gothic and Renaissance to Oriental and cottage.

Victorian Gothic, which followed the Gothic revival architecture of 1830 to 1850, is easily recognized by the Gothic arch shape, which appears in chair backs, mirrors, clocks, bed head-and-footboards, and the rosettes, crockets, and trefoil and quatrefoil motifs with which the furniture was embellished (see examples on pages 20 and 104–105).

Victorian Jacobean, simpler in style, was based, like Victorian Gothic, on designs in Charles Locke Eastlake's *Hints on Household Taste*. Parlor, bedroom, and dining room sets ornamented with gingerbread edging on shelves and aprons and flowers cut in outline were mass-produced from the 1870's until 1900.

Victorian Renaissance, based on the heavier, more ornate pieces of the Italian Renaissance, was perhaps the least felicitous of the revivals. Massive in scale and grandiose in concept, loaded with marble tops and ornate carving in which classic motifs mingled with flowers and fruit, it lingered from 1855 to 1875. The rooms on pages 21 and 22 are typical of this style.

Victorian Rococo, based on Louis XV, the lightest and most attractive and usable of the styles, was made from 1840 to 1860. Some of America's finest cabinetmakers like Belter, Elijah Galusha of Troy, and François Seignouret and Prudent Mallard of New Orleans produced custom-made furniture in this style. Some notable examples are shown in the restorations on pages 18–19 and 37. It was followed in the 1860's by another French revival, *Victorian Louis XVI*, but unfortunately the delicate lines and restrained classical ornamentation of the original were lost in the heavy-handed interpretation.

Victorian Oriental, the rage of the late nineteenth century, combined strong influences of the Far and Near East, like William Jennings Bryan's curio room on page 26. Lacquer, Chinese fretwork, bamboo, and bamboo-turned pieces were favored, and so was the Turkish corner with its deep upholstered and tufted ottomans and low octagonal tables with Moorish-arch bases, like the 1890's example on page 54.

Simplest of all was *Victorian Cottage*, the country-style furniture popular from the 1850's to the 1880's, especially the spool-turned pieces—whatnots, small tables and chairs, washstands and towel racks, and the Jenny Lind bed. Mostly, this furniture was plainly constructed of inexpensive softwoods, and painted or enameled in colors, often with stencil decoration, like that in the bedroom on page 24.

W

Wainscot chair. A carved wood panel-back chair common in England, France, and America during the sixteenth and seventeenth centuries. The name probably came from the high carved or inlaid back, reminiscent of wainscot paneling (see page 11, top).

Warming pan. An early form of heating pad, this wooden-handled pan, usually of brass with a decoratively pierced lid, held hot coals and warmed the cold beds of colonial homes.

Washstand. Unplumbed predecessor of the bathroom lavatory sink, this small table or cabinet was designed during the eighteenth century to hold the bedroom basin, ewer, and other toilet necessities. The elaborate marble-topped Victorian washstands are now much in demand as night stands or end tables, while the humbler versions in turned wood, which generally had a hole for the basin, are often turned into planters.

Weathervanes. First fashioned for the practical purpose of indicating the wind direction, wood and metal weathervanes became one of the earliest and most exuberant forms of American folk art, incredibly varied in design and craftsmanship. The earliest were merely silhouettes of fish, Indian archers, or running horses cut from sheet metal or carved from wood. Later, they were sand-cast in iron and sheathed with copper, and therefore became more sculptural in form. Wood weathervanes were usually painted for protection; metal ones might be left plain, painted, or gilded. The subject was often designed to suit the location: fish or gulls in coastal villages, trumpet-blowing angels on churches, locomotives on railroad stations. The current popularity and scarcity of old weathervanes has not only raised the price but also brought a rash of copies.

Westward Ho. Originally called Pioneer, this popular pressed glass pattern replete with such Western motifs as deer, bison, log cabins, and handles in the shape of Indians was inspired by the 1876 Centennial celebrations.

Willard clocks. Case, mantel, or wall clocks made, signed, and often dated by the Willards of Massachusetts—Benjamin, who set up a factory in Grafton in 1765; Aaron, who worked in Boston after 1790; and Simon, best known for the banjo clock he invented and patented in Roxbury in 1802.

Windsor chair. One of the most enduringly popular of all the simple country chairs. Introduced in England during the reign of Queen Anne and named for Windsor Castle, Windsor chairs were exported to the colonies in vast quantities. They were quickly adopted by local craftsmen and achieved their greatest fame and most graceful styling in America from 1725 to 1800. Originally, the chairs were made by wheelwrights, who laced the bentwood-back frames with spindles for support and pegged legs into saddle-shaped seats. The descriptive names of American Windsors serve to identify their many and varied shapes: hoop-back, comb-back, fan-back, bow-back, arch-back, arrow-back, rod-back, and low-back. There were also Windsor settees and rockers. Many examples are shown throughout this book.

Woven coverlets. The earliest woven coverlets of colonial times were hand loomed at home by women from yarn spun on a spinning wheel and dyed with vegetable dyes. They were a combination of wool and linen or cotton warp thread, usually in white, white and blue, or white and red. A more complicated type was the double-woven coverlet, with the reverse pattern underneath, made by itinerant professional weavers who used the household yarns and their own looms. After the Jacquard loom came into general use in the nineteenth century, the coverlets became more decorative and pictorial in design.

Bibliography

American Antiques

American Heritage History of American Antiques. New York: American Heritage Publishing Co., 1968.

American Heritage History of Colonial Antiques. New York: American Heritage Publishing Co., 1967.

Andrews, Edward Deming and Andrews, Faith. *Shaker Furniture*. New York: Dover Publications, 1937.

Aronson, Joseph. *The Encyclopedia of Furniture*. New York: Crown Publications, Inc., 1965.

Beck, Doreen. *Book of American Furniture*. New York: Hamlyn Publishing Co., 1973.

Burton, E. Milby. *Charleston Furniture, 1700–1825*. Columbia, S.C.: University of South Carolina Press, 1955.

Carpenter, Ralph E., Jr. *The Arts and Crafts of Newport, Rhode Island*. Rhode Island: Preservation Society of Newport County, 1954.

Colonial Williamsburg Foundation. *The Williamsburg Collection of Antique Furnishings*. New York: Holt, Rinehart & Winston, 1973.

De Jonge, Eric. *Country Things from the pages of the Magazine Antiques*. Princeton, N.J.: Pyne Press, 1973.

Fales, Dean A., Jr. *American Painted Furniture, 1660–1880*. New York: E. P. Dutton & Co. Inc., 1972.

Hinour, Hugh. *Cabinet Makers and Furniture Designers*. New York: G. P. Putnam's Sons, 1969.

Kovel, Ralph. *American Country Furniture, 1780–1875*. New York: Crown Publications Inc., 1965.

Lipman, Jean and Winchester, Alice. *The Flowering of American Folk Art (1776–1876)*. New York: The Viking Press, 1974.

Miller, Edgar G., Jr. *American Antique Furniture*. vols. I and II. New York: Dover Publications Inc., 1966.

Ormsbee, Thomas H. *Field Guide To Early American Antiques*. New York: Bonanza Books, 1950.

Schwartz, Marvin D. and Wade, Betsy. *The New York Times Book of Antiques*. New York: Quadrangle Books, 1972.

Shea, John G. *The American Shakers and Their Furniture*. New York: Van Nostrand Reinhold Co., 1971.

Winchester, Alice. *How To Know American Antiques*. New York: New American Library, 1951.

American Interiors

Antiques Magazine. *Great Houses*. Princeton, N.J.: Pyne Press, 1973.

Country Life. *The New Book of Smart Interiors*. American Home Corporation, 1937.

Chamberlain, Samuel and Chamberlain, Narcissa. *Southern Interiors of Charleston, South Carolina*. New York: Hastings House, 1956.

Genauer, Emily. *Modern Interiors*. New York: Illustrated Editions, 1939.

Germaine, Ina M. *Design For Decoration*. New York: Robert M. McBride & Co., 1946.

Gillies, Mary Davis. *All About Modern Decorating*. New York: Harper & Bros., 1942.

Guinness, Desmond and Sadler, Julius Trousdale, Jr. *Mr. Jefferson, Architect*. New York: Viking Press, 1973.

Hollister, Paul and Chamberlain, Samuel. *Beauport at Gloucester*. New York: Hastings House, 1951.

House & Garden's *Book of Interiors*. New York: Condé Nast & Co., 1920.

House & Garden's *Complete Guide To Interior Decorating*. New York: Simon & Schuster, 1950 and 1960.

Koch, Robert. *Louis C. Tiffany, Rebel In Glass*. New York: Crown Publishers, 1964.

Levin, Phyllis Lee. *Great Historic Houses of America*. New York: Coward-McCann, 1970.

Reif, Rita. *Treasure Rooms of America's Mansions, Manors and Houses*. New York: Coward-McCann, 1970.

Schwartz, Marvin D. *American Interiors, 1675–1885*. New York: Brooklyn Museum, 1968.

Sweeney, John A. *Winterthur Illustrated*. A Winterthur Book, 1963.

Williams, Henry Lionel and Williams, Ottalie K. *Great Houses of America*. New York: G. P. Putnam's Sons, 1966.

Wilson, José and Leaman, Arthur. *Decoration U.S.A*. New York: The Macmillan Co., 1965.

American Reproductions

Ethan Allen Treasury. New York: Ethan Allen, Inc.

Kittinger Company. *A Library of 18th Century English and American Designs*. Buffalo, N.Y.

————. *Old Dominion Collection*. Richmond, Va.

Williamsburg Reproductions. Williamsburg, Va.: Craft House.

Decorating Dictionaries

Dictionary of Design and Decorating. New York: The Viking Press, 1973.

Durant, Mary. *American Heritage Guide to Antiques*. New York: American Heritage Press, 1970.

Wilson, José and Leaman, Arthur. *Decorating Defined*. New York: Simon & Schuster, 1970.